THE COMPLETE
UXBRIDGE
ENGLISH
DICTIONRY

THE COMPLETE UXBRIDGE ENGLISH DICTIONARY is indebted
to Jack Dee, Jeremy Hardy, Rob Brydon, Sandi Toksvig, Bill Bailey,
Stephen Fry, Andy Hamilton, Tony Hawks, Harry Hill, Ross Noble,
Rory Bremner, Miles Jupp, Fred Macaulay, David Mitchell, Linda
Smith and Victoria Wood for their outstanding contributions to this
book, to Megan Landon for the research that made it possible, and
to Neal Townsend, Mark Oxenham and Graeme Garden for their
excellent illustrations.

3 5 7 9 10 8 6 4 2

Preface
20 Vauxhall Bridge Road
London
SW1V 2SA

Preface is part of the Penguin Random House group of companies
whose addresses can be found at global.penguinrandomhouse.com.

Copyright © Graeme Garden and Jon Naismith 2016

Graeme Garden and Jon Naismith have asserted their right to be identified as the authors
of this Work in accordance with the Copyright, Designs and Patents Act 1988.

First published by Preface in 2016

www.penguin.co.uk

A CIP catalogue record for this book is available from the British Library.

ISBN 9781848094970

Printed and bound in Great Britain by TJ International Ltd, Padstow, Cornwall

THE COMPLETE
UXBRIDGE
ENGLISH
DICTIONRY

Tim Brooke-Taylor

Barry Cryer

Graeme Garden

Jon Naismith

Iain Pattinson

Edited by Graeme Garden and Jon Naismith

UXBRIDGE
UNIVERSITY PRESS

Introduction

Whenever we come across an unfamiliar word, or whenever we need to check the true meaning or correct speling of a familiar word, where do we turn? We turn to the left. At least I do, because that's where my bookshelf is to be found. And on my bookshelf, nestling between *Adventures in Trigonometry* and the *I-Spy Book of Fruit Trees*, there sits my copy of this very book, *The Complete Uxbridge English Dictionary*.

The Complete Uxbridge English Dictionary (or CUED for short) is the jewel in the crown of the Uxbridge University Press (or UUP for short). The UUP (Uxbridge University Press) first produced the CUED (*Complete Uxbridge English Dictionary*) in the year 1834, and it has remained on the best-selling Dictionary list every year since that date until 1835.

When sales of *The Complete Uxbridge English Dictionary* (CUED) began to falter, the UUP (Uxbridge University Press) found itself under threat. However in 1836 it was rescued by the intervention of none other than Charles Dickens, the novelist. At that time the Dictionary (D) contained no less than 250 different words, and Dickens purchased all 250 of them for his own exclusive use, on condition that they were not to appear in any subsequent edition. Among the words he bought were 'pickwick' (a fussy or inquisitive person), 'dorrit' (a patch or shred of blanket) and 'scrooge' (to kiss with an excess of saliva).

Josiah Font loads 'antidisestablishmentarianism'
into the Uxbridge University Press (UUP)

With the money from the sale of words to Dickens, the Uxbridge University Press (UUP) could afford to employ a full-time lexicographer to expand and improve the CUED (*Complete Uxbridge English Dictionary*) and in the hands of Josiah Font it blossomed into the volume that you hold in your hands today.

Now, thanks to *The Complete Uxbridge English Dictionary* (CUED) you no longer need to appear to be a chuzzlewit.

N.V.Q. de Ploma

Dean, Vice-Chancellor, Remedial Embroidery

fig.1 Archive

A4
A road made of paper

Abacus
Swedish swear word

Abatement
Downstairs storage area used by man with sinus trouble

Abattoir
Three-in-a-bed in a monastery

Aberdare
To challenge Benny, Björn, Agnetha and Anni-Frid

Aberystwyth
A little me time while listening to 'Dancing Queen'

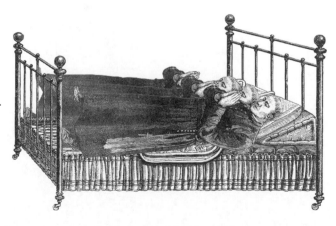

fig.2 Abattoir

Aa

Abigail
A large wind

Abort
Sea-faring vessel from the Midlands

Abscond
To steal someone's cream tea

Academic
An outbreak of clarinet playing

Academy
School for complete bastards

Acapulco
Unaccompanied
Mexican singing

fig.3 Abscond

Accomplish
A drunken sidekick

Acne
Borough in East London

Acolyte
Easy-listening clarinet music

Acoustic
A Scottish cattle prod

Acropolis
Italian for 'short back and sides if you'd be so kind'

Acupuncture
Very deliberate tyre slashing

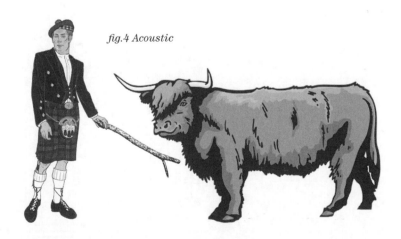

fig.4 Acoustic

Aa

Adamant
The very first male ant

Adder
Tasteless boast

Admission
Yet another sequel for Tom Cruise

Aerobic
Chocolate biro

Aerofoil
Chocolate wrapper

Aerospace
Room for more chocolate

Aetiology
The study of food

fig.5 Adamant

fig.6 Agog

Adamant – Alcopops

Affiliation
Affair with a horse

Aficionados
Charity home for orphan fish

Aggregate
Farming scandal

Agog
A half-finished Jewish temple

Albino
Spanish kids' comic

Alcopops
Alcoholic dads

fig. 7 Affiliation

Aa

Alfalfa
A dominant male with a stammer

Algebra
A brassiere made out of kelp

Algorithm
Former Vice President on drums

Alimony
With lemon

Alkaline
A queue at Alcoholics Anonymous

Alligator
Someone who accuses you of things

Allocate
How you greet the Duchess
of Cambridge

fig.8 Algebra

fig.9 Alligator

Alone and forlorn
A borrowed mowing machine

Alpaca
What Italians say when they go on holiday

Alpenhorn
Muesli with dirty bits

Already
Suffering from sunburn

Altercation
  [1] To change holiday plans
  [2] Holiday for a vicar

Aluminium
A religious chorus for metal workers

Ambulate
A hearse

fig.10 Ambulate

Aa

Amish
Rather like an arm

Amstrad
Amateur violinist

Analogy
Something that makes you itchy and sneezy

Analyse
To examine someone's backside

Angiogram
Irish folk singer

Animate
To grow too fond of your pets

Annex
Captain Mark Phillips

fig.11 Analyse

Announce
28 grams

Annunciate
To take holy orders loudly and clearly

Antelope
To run off with your mother's sister

Anticlimax
Excited female relative

Antiquarian
A very old fish tank

Antique
The shrill cry of the ant

Aperitif
Cockney dentures

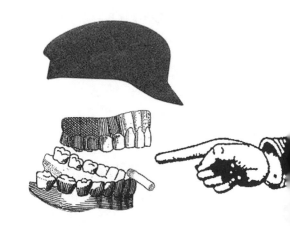

fig.12 Aperitif

Aa

Apex
Gorilla's wristwatch

Apocalypse
Disastrous collagen injection

Apollo
Roman god of chickens

Apology
The study of iPad applications

Appendectomy
What Ant shouts when he wants a biro

Appetite
Cheerfully drunk

Approximate
A mistress

Arboretum
A dockside restaurant

fig.13 Apocalypse

Arcade
Noah's charity

Arcane
Liverpudlian bamboo

Archery
Lying under oath and at all other times

Archive
Where Noah kept his bees

Argy-bargy
Owner of a narrow boat in
Buenos Aires

Arizona
The person that Arry
belongs to

Armature
An old pirate

fig.14 Appetite

Aa

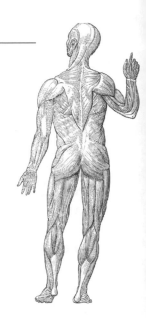

Aromatic
A handy gadget used by Robin Hood

Arrest
That long stick thing they use in snooker

Arresting
Jamaican bed

Arsehole
Cry of delight on hearing Marvin Gaye

fig.15 Arsenal

Arsenal
The whole body

Arsenic
Result of sitting on a razor blade

Arson
Seated

fig.16 Arsenic

Artefact
Pretentious statistic

Artery
Shooting arrows at paintings

Artichoke
To suppress a cough while
at the theatre

Article
To tease a pirate

fig. 17 Artery

Artistry
History of art

Asbestos
Greek Anti-Social Behaviour Order

fig. 18 Asbestos

Aa

ASBO
Is courting

Asperger's syndrome
A tendency to overuse laxatives

Aspersion
Iranian donkey

Asphalt
Constipation

Aspic
Don't do that

Aspire
The pointy bit on a church

Assailant
A cut-price insect

Assassination
An arrangement to meet a donkey

fig.19 Assailant

Assert
A sure winner

Asshole
Suddenly remembering the capital of South Korea

Assimilate
To pretend to be a donkey

Asterisk
The chances of being hit by an asteroid

Asthmatic
Electric bidet

Asymmetry
Place where you bury stiffs

Atomiser
Someone who hoards his molecules

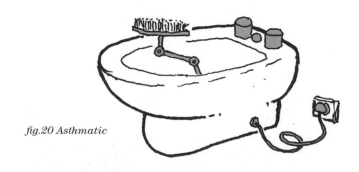

fig.20 Asthmatic

Aa

Atrophy
Something you win at sport

Audi A4
What you say when you drop a heavy ream
of paper on your foot

Autobiography
A car service book

fig.21 Atrophy

Autocue
Traffic jam

Automat
October headwear

Avocado
To do one's supermarket shopping online

Avoidable
What a cow with a headache does

AWOL
A dyslexic owl

OW!

fig.22 Audi A4

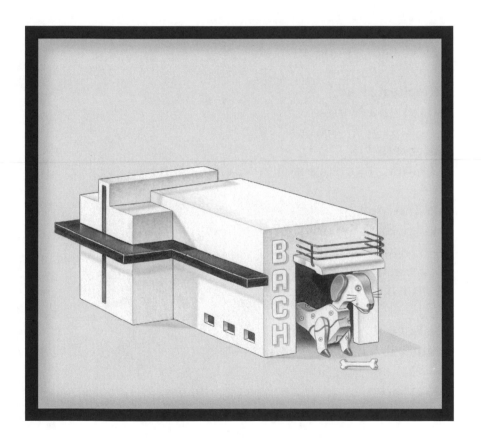

fig.23 Bauhaus

Bb

B&B
A hive with a population of two

Bacchanalian
To bet on a Martian

Bacteria
Returning more upset than when you left

Badminton
Dodgy English porcelain

Baguette
A little bag

Bakery
Rather like a baker

Balalaika
A fan of *Swan Lake*

fig.24 Bacchanalian

B&B – Banquette

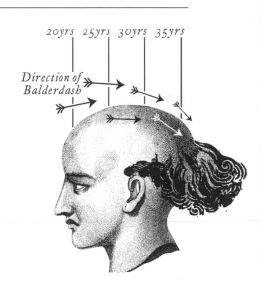

Balderdash
A rapidly receding hairline

Ball-bearing
The side a gentleman dresses

Balloon
An inflatable Belgian

Baltic
Involuntary testicular spasm

fig.25 Balderdash

Baltimore
To ask for seconds in an Indian restaurant

Bandaging
Rolling Stones

Banquette
A tiny shag

fig.26 Baguette

Bb

Banshee
Gentlemen's club

Baptise
Neckwear made of bread rolls

Baptist
A junior hamburger chef

Barbecue
Long wait for a haircut

Barcode
A poem by a dog

Barman
1. A superhero who takes a very long time to notice anybody
2. A sheep impressionist

Barney
Rather like a barn

fig.27 Baptise

Banshee – Battleaxe

fig.28 Bathos

Barometric
Euro gardening aid

Barrel-organ
Brewer's droop

Barrier
Even more like Barry than Barry is

Bathos
The anticlimactic musketeer

Battery
Where you leave your bat when you go on holiday

Battleaxe
A boon for constipated bats

fig.29 Barbecue

Bb

Bauhaus
1. Buckingham Palace
2. Dog kennel

Bazaar
Barry the pirate

Bear-baiting
Nude fishing

Bearings
Yogi's jewellery

Beaten
A posh school for bees

Beatitude
Stroppy mood common in teenage insects

Bedlam
A very special sheep

fig.30 Bearings

Bauhaus – Beguile

Beehive
What Australian
teachers tell you to do

Beetroot
Scottish term for a
second class trout

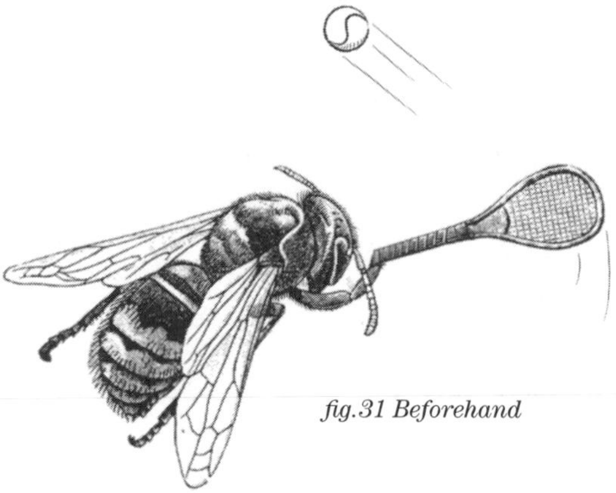

fig.31 Beforehand

Beforehand
Insect tennis stroke

Befuddle
A tight group of cattle

Begat
What you wear on a big 'ed

Beginnings
A century at Lords

Beguile
A very broad church

fig.32 Begat

Bb

Behemoth
An insect that makes holes in your jumpers and then fills them with honey

Beholder
To sing with 'Slade'

Benign
What it'll be after eight

Bequest
A bee hunt

Bespoke
How baby bees are made

Beware
Clothing for bees

Biased
Having four buttocks

fig.33 Beware

fig.34 Benign

Biceps
Sexually ambivalent mushrooms

Bicker
Like a ballpoint only more so

Bicycle
  [1.] A double-headed corn-cutter
  [2.] An icicle that swings both ways

Bidet
Two days before D-Day

Bigamist
A larger than usual fog

Bigamy
That shows magnanimity on my part

Bigotry
A lumberjack's boast

fig.35 Bicycle

Bb

Bijoux
Source of kosher honey

Bile
Australian bundle of hay

Binmen
People who were male but are now female

Biology
The science of why women shop

Biopsy
An organic gypsy

Biosphere
To purchase a ball

fig.36 Bijoux

fig.37 Binmen

Bipolar
A bear; one day he's grizzly, the next
day he's all white

Birkenhead
Merseyside body snatchers

Biro
To purchase fish eggs

Bishopric
Unpopular member of the clergy

Bison
What Hollywood stars go to Africa for

Bizarre
Ruler of the Russian bees

Blame
Walking with a blimp

fig.38 Blame

Bb

Blatter
Someone who very nearly gets away
with it

Bleach
A hole in the Great Wall of China

Blemish
The official language of Belgium

fig.39 Blistered

Blistered
A very satisfying bowel movement

Blistering
Someone you enjoy calling on the phone

Bloating
Jamaican whistle

Blogger
Computer-literate lumberjack

fig.40 Bombardier

Bloodshed
A cheap place to get a transfusion

Boa constrictor
South African truss

Boing
A manufacturer of rubber aircraft

Bollocks
Unsuccessful botox

Bombardier
An overly aggressive form of culling

Bonus
What bankers get when they handle money

Boomerang
Show displeasure to a pudding

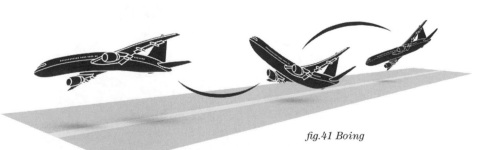

fig.41 Boing

Bb

Bordeaux
To weary a deer

Bordello
Blasé greeting

Botham
Where Gatman lives

Botox
A seafaring bullock

Bouffant
To heckle a typeface

Boulangerie
To heckle underwear

Boundary
Ungentlemanly behaviour

Boutique
To heckle wood

fig.42 Botox

fig.43 Brandish

Bordeaux – Bridget

Brandish
What Sean Connery has for a nightcap

Brandy
Having a high sex drive and bow legs

Bratwürst
Dennis the Menace

Brexit
Breakfast cereal laxative

Briar patch
Something to help you
overcome your craving
for thickets

Bridget
A small bridge

fig.44 Boutique

Bb

Brisket
A fast moving old man

Britanny
A bit like Britain

Broadband
  [1.] No fatties please
  [2.] Fat musicians, e.g.
    The Obesity Rollers

Brocade
Medical assistance
for badgers

Bronchodilator
A very old horse

Brouhaha
A cup of tea that tastes funny

Buccaneer
What American pirates
pay for piercing

Buffalo
Popular greeting at a nudist camp

fig.45 Brisket

Buggery
The study of insects

Bulletin
I've been shot

Bullfrog
Frenchman who talks rubbish

Bumblebee
Reserve Beadle

Bumbling
Jewellery for the buttocks

fig.46 Buggery

fig.47 Brocade

Bb

Bumpkin
A serviette used in the lavatory

Bumpy
A very loose bowel movement

Bungalow
Small building used for Berlusconi parties

Bungee
The one after bun 'F'

Bunny
Rather like a bun

Buoyant
Adam Ant's son

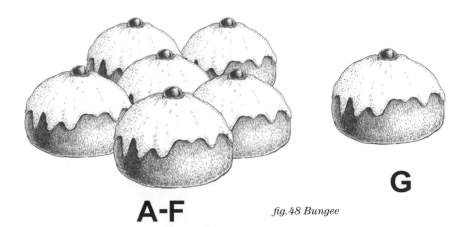

A-F   *fig.48 Bungee*   **G**

Burnish
A bit like a burn

Bustard
A very rude omnibus driver

Buttercup
Face down

Butternut
Heads or tails

Buttonhole
One of the more uncomfortable body waxes

Buttresses
Especially lustrous bottom hair

Buzzard
Energetic panel game

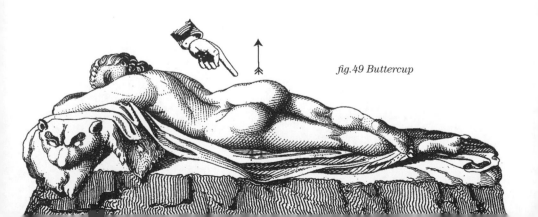

fig.49 Buttercup

fig.50 Childhood

Cabaret
A wide range of available taxis

Cabbage
The opinions of taxi drivers

Cabin
The taxi's arrived

Cabriolet
A popular brand of milk chocolate

Cacti
Rubbish neckwear

fig.51 Cacti

Caddy
Rather like a cad

Cadillac
Having to carry your own golf clubs

Caesarean section
Part of a salad

Cc

Cage fighter
Angry hamster

Campervan
Van with more sequins than most

Canapé
Scottish inability to settle bills

Canary
Extremely hirsute

Candid
Past tense of 'can do'

Cannelloni
Scots refusal to give one an overdraft

fig.52 Canary

Cage fighter – Cantankerous

Cannibal
Shrewd Aberdeen Angus

Cannibalistic
A Geordie missile

Canoodle
To fondle in a small boat

Canopy
Scots complaint

Cantaloupe
Unable to run off and get married

Cantankerous
Chain of shops that sell tanks

fig.53 Cannibalistic

fig.54 Cantankerous

Cc

Canteen
One who has reached the age of consent

fig.55 Caramel

Canticle
The only skill listed on Mr Tickle's CV

Cantilever
The switch on an electric horse

Capable
Two things you need to be a matador

Capsule
Better than Christmas

Caramel
Toffee with one hump

Cardamom
Mother's Day card

fig.56 Carpentry

Cardiac
Somebody who knows a hell of a lot about cardigans

Cardiology
The study of knitwear

Carmelite
Entry-level Buddhism

Carpentry
A 'way in' for ornamental fish

Carping
Imitating a fish

Cashew
A nut that makes you sneeze

fig.57 Carping

Cc

Castanets
What Italian fishermen do

Castigate
To have a nasty accident
climbing into a field

Catacomb
Feline grooming service

fig.58 Catastrophe

Catalyst
A three-legged moggie

Catastrophe
[1.] Feline punctuation
[2.] Feline Rear of the Year Award

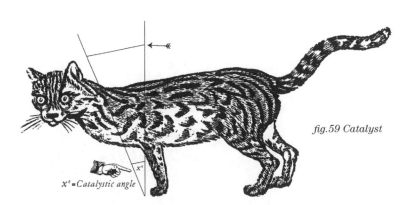

$x° = $ *Catalystic angle*

fig.59 Catalyst

Catatonic
Medicine for your pussy

Catchphrase
Howzat!

Catharsis
Bums on seats at mass

Cathartic
When the bag freezes

Caustic
Good heavens, a twig!

Celery
A bit like a cellar

Celtic
A prison for fleas

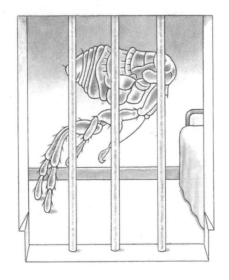

fig.60 Celtic

Cc

Cemented
The world's least popular cuddly toy

Cenotaph
A Welsh laxative

Cesspit
Brad's unsavoury brother

Chagrin
To smile broadly during intercourse

Chairs
A toast by the Queen

Chaise longue
That woman's very tall

Chameleon
Half camel, half lion

fig.61 Chaise longue

Champagne
To pretend to be hurt

Charabancs
The cleaning lady's a goer

Charlady
Joan of Arc

Chary
Rather like a chair

Chatanooga
Talk about confectionery

Château
Cat's piss

Chatelaine
Couldn't get home in time

fig.62 Chatelaine

Cc

Chauffeur
What can happen when you exit
your car without knickers

Cheapskate
A fish that does budgie impressions

Chepstow
A digit at the end of a
gentleman's foot

Cherish
Rather like a chair

Childhood
Very young gangster

Chinchilla
An air-conditioned beard

fig.63 Cheapskate

fig.64 Chinchilla

Chauffeur – Ciabatta

Chipmunk
A friar

Chiropractice
Getting ready to go to Egypt

fig.65 Chipmunk

Choosy
A bit like toffee

Chutney
No man's land between Chiswick and Putney

Chutzpah
A character in Shakespeare's *Henry V*

Ciabatta
The wookie in *Star Wars*

fig.66 Chiropractice

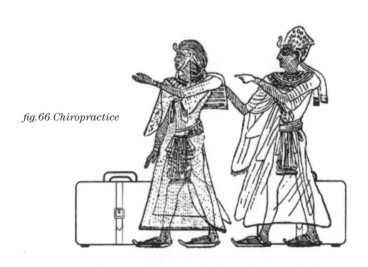

Cc

Circular
Performing vampire

Circumflex
To cut the end off a piece of wire

Circumnavigation
Jewish ritual on a cruise liner

fig.67 Circular

Circumspect
The point of view of a rabbi

Cistern
A toilet painted by Michelangelo

Claimant
An insect that's had
an accident at work

Clamour
Mallet for opening
clams

fig.68 Cistern

Clamp
To applaud while
wearing gloves

Claptrap
A condom

Clarify
To refine the
Grundys

Clarity
A bit like red wine

fig.69 Claustrophobia

Claustrophobia
Irrational fear of being stuck in a lift
with Father Christmas

Clematis
Not quite what you're trying to find

Climate
First instruction at mountaineering school

Cc

Cloister
A pretentious clam

Co-opt
Brainwashed by a leading supermarket chain

Cockaleekie
Prostate problem

Cocker spaniel
At your peril

Cockney
Damage to the patella from a long penis

Cockroach
Particularly nasty personal infestation

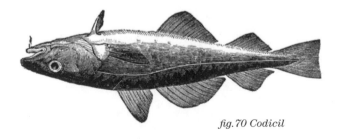

fig. 70 Codicil

Cocoa bean
An ex-clown

Coconut
Chocoholic

Codicil
  [1.] This fish is unwell
  [2.] Buffalo Bill's window box

Coffee
A person who is coughed upon

Cogitate
Art gallery for the elderly

Cognac
To deceive a long-haired cow

Coiffeur
A pretentious drinker

fig. 71 Cocoa bean

Cc

Coincidental
Having matching teeth

Coitus interruptus
Deck games on the
Titanic

Colander
Mr and Mrs Sell

Colgate
Scandal involving our
pianist

Collier
Like a collie but even
more so

Colliery
Sort of like a collie but
even more so

Collusion
A well-planned collision

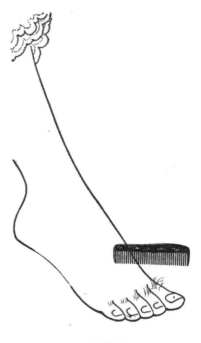

fig. 72 Comatose

Collywobbles
A three-legged
sheepdog

Colonnade
A fizzy enema

Colony
Like him on the piano

Comatose
[1.] Foot's gone dead
[2.] What a beautician
does to a lady with
a lot of unwanted hair

Combat
An aggressive marsupial

Comforting
Jamaican lost property

Commonplace
Essex

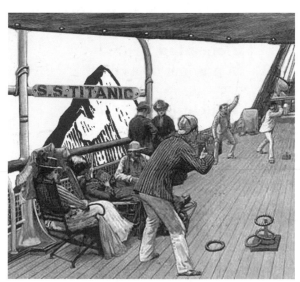

fig.73 Coitus interruptus

Cc

Conceited
A prisoner on a chair

Conclude
An obscenely shaped nose

Concourse
Lessons in swindling

Concubine
A porcupine with a big nose

Concurrent
An object that looks like a raisin, but isn't

Condense
To fool the stupid

Condescending
A prisoner in a lift

Condescension
Patronising droplets on a window

fig. 74 Condominium

Condom
Tory tax exile

Condominium
A birth control device made from metal

Confirm
An aroused prisoner

Congo
Constipation

Consent
Fake perfume

Context
A prison library book

Contextualise
To send fraudulent text messages

Contraband
US-backed counter-revolutionary
orchestra

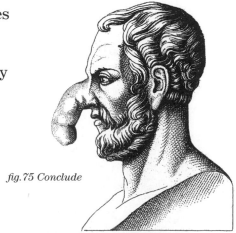

fig. 75 Conclude

Cc

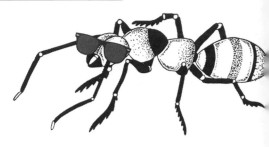

Contradiction
How Nicaraguan rebels
speak

fig.76 Coolant

Conurbation
What convicts do alone
in their cells late at night

Coolant
An ant wearing sunglasses

Copper
More like a policeman

Copulate
The time it takes the police to show
up in an emergency

Coquette
A tiny little penis

Cormorant
An ant who likes a mild curry

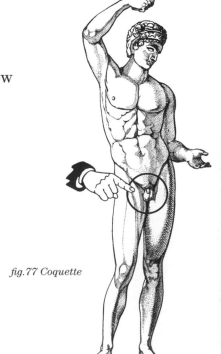

fig.77 Coquette

Contradiction – Cortisone

Cormorants
Good heavens, extra insects!

Cornucopia
Coming to terms with your foot ailment

Correspondent
Sent into depression by *Coronation Street*

Corridor
Entrance to the Rover's Return

Corrode
Good heavens, a lyric poem!

Corsage
Blimey, it's a copper!

Cortisone
What the solitary angler did

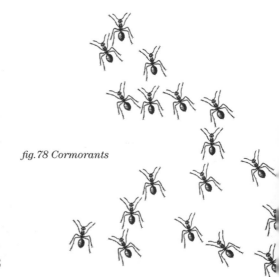

fig. 78 Cormorants

Cc

Counterpane
Someone working in the Post Office

Countryside
To kill Piers Morgan

County Down
A Chinese space launch

Coupé
A wig for a car

Courgette
Look, an aeroplane!

Courtesy
Dog to visit

Coypu
What is done
behind a bush at a
picnic

fig.79 Coupé

Crab-apple
An apple that falls sideways from a tree

Crackerjack
A device for raising biscuits

Cranium
Gymnasium for cranes

Crèche
A car accident in Woking

Credit crunch
The world's worst-selling
breakfast cereal

Crème brûlée
The crematorium's on fire

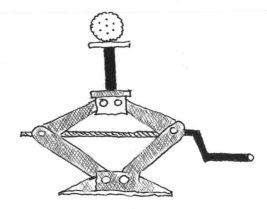

fig.80 Crackerjack

Crepuscular
A pancake that's spent too long in the gym

Crescendo
Termination of child care

Cc

Crocus
A foul-mouthed bird

Croquette
A tiny little crocodile

Cross-country
Iran

Crucifix
Religious adhesive

Crudity
A sea shanty

Cruise control
Scientology

Crumpet
Small animal made of dough

SH*T!

BL**DY!

T*SSER!

fig.81 Crocus

Crocus – Culotte

Crystalline
Go too far in New Zealand

Crystallise
A retirement gift for Lord Nelson

Cubic
A biro that you can play snooker with

fig.82 Cross-country

Cubicle
A square bicycle

Cuckold
So chilly you stutter

Culotte
Post Office

fig.83 Cubic

Cc

Curate
A doctor

Curator
Someone who assesses snooker equipment

Curlicue
Welsh dog

Cursory
Where small children learn to swear

Custard
To swear after stepping in something

Cuticle
[1] Sexual harassment at the Post Office
[2] A rather nice testicle

Cyanide
To exhale noisily then conceal oneself

Cyrillic
Similar to Cyril

fig.84 Curate

fig.85 Domineering

Dd

Dace
What the Queen uses to play
board games

Daewoo
Host of *Supermarket Sweep*

Damnation
Holland

Dandelion
A big camp cat

Dashboard
Selectors for the 100 metres

Database
Place where Lonely Hearts hang out

Daunting
Sunrise in Jamaica

fig.86 Dandelion

fig.87 Damnation

Dayglo
Shiny Spaniard

Debasement
De room under de
ground floor

Debrief
Remove underwear

Decade
Ant

Decadence
Ten times as stupid

Decaff
Where you get de coffee

Decant
All-purpose TV presenter

Debating
Where ships anchor in Jamaica

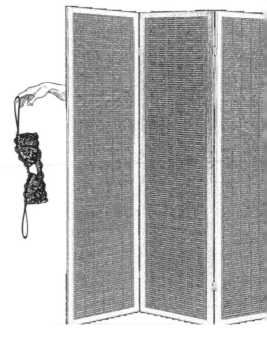

fig.88 Debrief

Dd

Decanter
What Jack does before
he breaks into a gallop

Decease
To stop stopping

Decentralise
Jack, the cyclops

Decrease
Do the ironing

Decreased
Jack in hysterics

Deduce
What you get when you squeeze de lemon

Defamatory
Hard of hearing but still frisky

Defeat
Jack's party trick

fig.89 Defamatory

Defective
Policeman with a speech impediment

Defibrillate
To interpret the meaning of Jeffrey Archer

Definite
Street slang for 'hard of hearing'

Deft
Absolutely mad

Defunct
To have had one's sense of rhythm removed

Defuse
De circuit breaker in de plug

Dehydrate
De cost of skinning an animal

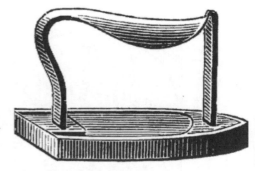

fig.90 Decrease

Dd

Delaware
To have seen *Only Fools And Horses*

Delegate
Scandal involving a food shop

Deliberate
To lock up

Delicate
A self-assembly food shop

Delighted
Extinguished

Delivery
De outfits of de palace staff

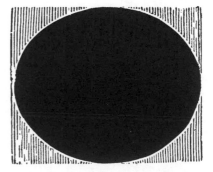

fig.91 Delighted

Demand
Recently widowed

Demister
Castration device

Demistifier
Retired magician

Demonic
Her Majesty de Queen

fig.92 *Demistifier*

Dentist
Someone who repairs car bodywork

Dependable
A confident swimmer

Dependent
De hole made by de biro

Depressant
The ant who works for the *Daily Mail*

Dd

Derelict
Pleasant experience in Ireland

Descant
An ant with an office job

Descent
To remove the smell

Deserted
The pudding's done a runner

fig.93 Diabetes

Detonation
A country that owes a lot of money

Diabetes
To drop dead while making eyes at an insect

Diabolical
A Welsh make of wine

fig.94 Deserted

Derelict – Dichotomy

Diagnose
A proboscis which starts on the top right of the face and finishes on the bottom left

Diagnostic
Welshman unsure if God exists

Dialogue
An awful piece of wood

Diamante
Way to start letter to wartime Field Marshal

Diarrhoea
Ugly bum

Diary
Disappointing ecstasy tablet

Dichotomy
Surgical procedure for the removal of an unwanted Welshman

fig.95 Descant

Dd

Dictaphone
Someone you don't like calling

Dictating
To leak milk from an unusual place

Dictator
An amusingly shaped root vegetable

Dictionary
The rude version of Pictionary

Diffident
Novelty toothpaste

Digest
Welsh clown

Digression
Welsh fighting talk

Diktat
Shoddy condom

fig.96 Dictator

Dilate
To live long

Dilatory
Conservative sex aid

Dildo
Pickled pastry

Dilute
Welsh musical instrument

Diphthong
Underwear fondue

Direct
Ruined by a Welshman

Direction
An aroused Welshman

fig.97 Digest

Dd

Disability
To criticise ability

Disappear
To insult a lord

Disconsolate
A particular embassy

Discount
To make clear which member of the nobility
you are talking about

Discover
Jamaican for duvet

Disdain
To be rude to someone from Denmark

Disgruntled
A pig with laryngitis

fig.98 Discount

Disability – Diverging

Disgusted
The wind has dropped

Disillusion
To slag off the work of
David Copperfield

Dismiss
To be rude to teacher

Dispersal
To slag off a washing powder

fig.99 Dismiss

Dissuade
To insult Hush Puppies

Ditto
The Marx Brother who got fired
because he was too samey

Diverging
Unsuccessful Welsh
lothario

fig.100 Disgruntled

Dd

Docile
Where they keep the medications in a supermarket

Doctrine
Your GP has arrived

Dodo
A repeat of *The Simpsons*

Dog pound
Seventh of a human pound

Dogma
A bitch

Dogmatic
A dog without a clutch

Doldrums
Percussion for the unemployed

fig.101 Dogma

Docile – Downsize

Domineering
An earring shaped like a domino

Dominion
A baker's assistant

Doodah
A cool pirate

Dossier
A terribly posh tramp

Doughnut
Eccentric millionaire

Download
Aftermath of a heavy Indian meal

Downsize
Unit of feather measurement

fig.102 Dominion

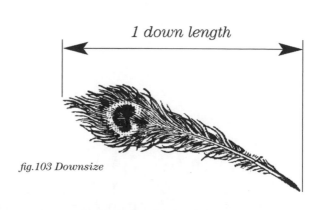

1 down length

fig.103 Downsize

Dd

Dreadlocks
Fear of canals

Dressage
A cross-dressing police officer

Dubai
Debbie from Birmingham

Dukedom
Aristocratic birth control aid

Dullard
A boring duck

Dumbstruck
A white van

Dumpling
A small dump

Mallard ☞

Dullard ☞

fig.104 Dullard

Dunderhead
Exclamation by a sculptor after he has finished the top part of a bust

Dunstable
To have shaved

Dynamite
To take a flea out for lunch

Dyspepsia
The inability to distinguish between different brands of cola

fig.105 Dynamite

fig.106 Enrage

Earache
Yorkshire expression of surprise at seeing garden implement

Early
Rather like an earl

Earwig
A present for someone who's got everything

Easily
Like an easel

Eastertide
What goes in and out on the Yorkshire coast

Ebola
Yorkshire 'at

Eclipse
Devices for holding electronic documents together

Economist
Cheap fog

fig.107 Earwig

Ee

Ecstatic
Now moving

Eczema
No longer your mother

Edam
Mild Yorkshire expletive

Eerie
A bit like an ear

fig.108 Ecstatic

Eeyore
A prostitute who advertises on the internet

Effigy
Colin's musical range

Egalitarian
One who only eats birds of prey

Egocentric
The yolk

Egregious
King of the eggs

Egret
An apology sent by computer

Eiderdown
A sad duck

fig.109 Egregious

Ejaculate
Yorkshire greeting to husband on
delayed return from t'mill

Elate
A Spanish rowing crew

Elegy
An inflammatory reaction
to poetry

Elemental
Spanish village idiot

Elevenses
A Welsh bullfighting
family

fig.110 Elemental

Ee

Elfish
Spanish seafood

Eliminate
Yorkshire exclamation on seeing a fizzy drink

Email
Yorkshire for 'the postman's

Emboss
To promote to the top

Emeralds
Green piles

Emotions
Virtual dumps

Enamour
What you use to bang nails in

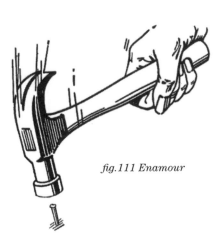

fig.111 Enamour

Encounter
Where they sell chicken in the supermarket

Encyclopaedia
To be sexually attracted to small bikes

Endorse
Loser in the Grand National

Engineer
A parking space next to your house

Enquire
A group of singing chickens from the East End

Enrage
A row about poultry in the East End

fig.112 Endorse

Ee

Entente cordiale
A happy French camper

Entities
An indeterminate number of breasts

Entrechat
A bisexual cat

Enunciate
To take holy orders loudly and clearly

Epilogue
A cheerful piece of wood

Equidistant
An ant who's been slagged off by a horse

Equip
Internet witticism

Erectile
Where they keep the
Viagra in the supermarket

fig.113 Epilogue

fig.114 Ersatz

Ersatz
Somerset milliner

Esplanade
To attempt an explanation while drunk

Ethics
The place where girls with white stilettos live

Etiquette
What you get for a parking offence
in South Africa

Eureka
BO

Euthanasia
Young people in China

Evacuate
What you say to a Yorkshireman
who's just swallowed a hoover

fig.115 Eureka

Ee

Evanescence
A Welshman who glows in the dark

Evil
The opposite of 'evon't'

Excalibur
Former drinker of non-alcoholic beer

Exceed
A plant

Exchequer
Someone who counts the kisses on an email

Exclaim
Alimony

Excommunication
Drunk texts from an old girlfriend

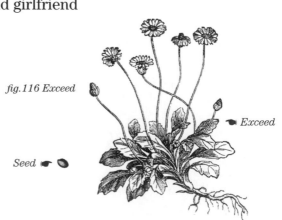

fig.116 Exceed

Exceed

Seed

Excrete
Formerly resident on a Greek island

Expert
Former Page 3 girl

Expense
Old money

Expensive
No longer thoughtful

Explain
Concorde

Extemporary
Permanent

Extension
Bumping into an old flame
with your current partner

Extort
Having left school

fig.117 Expense

Ee

Extractor fan
Former lover of
agricultural equipment

Eye-glass
A goblet made by Apple

Eyebrow
Digital forehead

Eyeliner
A big ship made by Apple

Eyeopener
Batsman made by Apple

Eyesore
A carpentry tool made by Apple

fig.118 Eye-glass

fig.119 Eyesore

fig.120 Flatulence

Ff

Faculty
Cockney for 'there's no more PG Tips'

Faint
Vulgar version of 'fisn't'

Fajitas
What they use gas for in Newcastle

Fallacy
Amusingly shaped

Falsetto
Fake ice cream

Farage
A garage that won't accept Volkswagens

Farcical
A bike that makes you look
stupid

fig.121 Farcical

Farting
Something a long way from
an Irishman

Fastidious
A very ugly sprinter

fig.122 Fastidious

Faux pas
He's not your dad

Feckless
An Irish virgin

Fecund
The one before 'fird'

Fedex
Blimey, you got fat since we
broke up

Felching
A successful insurance
claim after tripping on the
pavement

fig.123 Felching

Ff

Felony
Stumbled and landed on leg joint

Female
Chemical name for Iron Man

Fervent
A device required when tumble-drying cats

Fiasco
Unsuccessful wall painting

Fibre-optics
1. The healthy alternative to eye candy
2. Bartenders' measures for muesli

Fibreboard
Fed up with a healthy diet

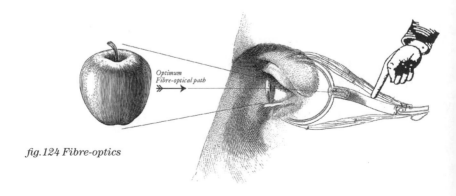

fig.124 Fibre-optics

Fibula
A small lie

Fiddledeedee
Jack's violin

Fielding
To find a bell in the dark

Figurine
Butter substitute made from figs

fig.125 Fervent

Filibuster
Clumsy vet

Filipino
Brian's lesser known brother

Fillip
A great boost for the Queen

fig.126 Filibuster

Ff

Filofax
Pastry so thin you can send it by telephone

Finalise
A better class of untruths

Finesse
A lady from Finland

First
The one before 'fecund'

Fish
A bit like an F

Fishiest
Someone who doesn't believe in cod

Five-aside
To kill a boy band

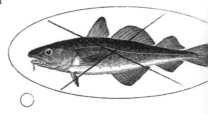

fig.127 Fishiest

Fixate
To sabotage a rowing crew

Flabbergasted
Appalled at your weight gain

Flagrant
A tramp with a whip

Flashpoint
Hampstead Heath

Flatterer
A rolling pin

fig.128 Flagrant

Flattery
Where you leave your flat when you go on holiday

Flatulence
An emergency vehicle that picks you up after you have been run over by a steam roller

Flaubert
Andy Capp's stash of Polaroids of the wife

Ff

Flemish
Prone to spitting

Flippant
An insect that maximises its expense claims by re-designating its second home

fig.129 Flippertygibbet

Flippertygibbet
Dolphin gallows

Flirt
A vehicle driven by a Geordie milkman

Floral
Foreplay on the carpet

Florida
More red in the face

fig.130 Flotilla

Flotilla
An amphibious ape

Fly tipping
Giving gratuities to insects

Foaming
Dodgy Chinese porcelain

Foible
Something coughed up by a New York cat

Follicle
A tiny little ruin built on a small hill

Fondue
An affectionate sheep

Foodstuff
The meat is hard to cut

fig.131 Fondue

Ff

Footstool
What you get when you step in dog poo

Forbearing
A group of pregnant women

Forebear
Look out, there's a bear on the golf course!

Forebears
A really terrible night for Goldilocks

Forecast
To have cutlery protruding from your posterior

Foreskin
To compel a relative

fig.132 Forbearing

Fornication
Communication between golfers

Forswear
Army uniform

Fossilise
When it's too late for glasses

Founder member
Result of rummaging in your Y-fronts

Foxglove
Basil Brush

Foxtrots
Bowel disorder brought on by hunting

Francophile
Spanish dictator's medical records

Frankincense
To annoy Frank

fig.133 Forecast

Ff

Freebie
An unattached insect

Freemasonry
To liberate concrete

Frigate
A ship that nobody cares about

Frogmarch
Third month in the French calendar

Frog-spawn
Blue movies for the French

Frowning
Herr Ning's wife

Frugal
A search engine for fruit

fig.134 Freebie

Fulfil
To fill full

Fundamentalist
To give money to David Icke

Funding
A humorous door chime

Fungal
Good female company

Fungi
Good male company

Furnish
A bit like a fern

Fuselage
Not many that big

Fungi

Fungal

fig.135 Fungal and Fungi

fig.136 Guacamole

Gandhi
A bow-legged ventriloquist

Gangster
A criminal pasty

Gap
In which a ventriloquist serves his burger

Garden hose
Graeme's lady friends

Gargoyle
An olive-flavoured mouthwash

Gasket
Where a ventriloquist puts his shopping

fig.137 Gargoyle

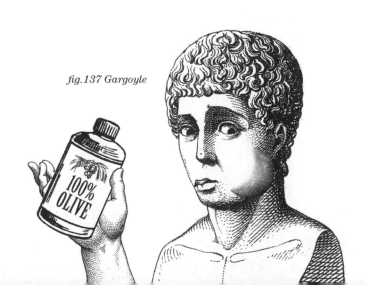

Gg

Gastric
Lighting a fart

Gastric band
A wind ensemble

Gastronome
A diminutive foodie

Gastronomy
The study of Michelin stars

Gateau
A French ventriloquist's boat

Gaucho
Argentinian Marx brother

Gazette
A baby antelope

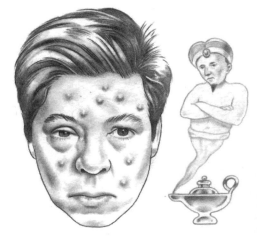

fig.138 Genealogy

Gear
What ventriloquists drink in pubs

Gearstick
Glue for clothes

Geiger counter
Where to buy geigers in a
department store

Gelatine
A device for cutting the heads
off Jelly Babies

fig. 139 Gelatine

Genealogy
What makes Aladdin sneeze

Genteel
Chivalrous fish

Gentile
Where they keep the men's
products in a supermarket

fig. 140 Genteel

Gg

Geranium
The cry of the Parachute Regiment's
flower arranging display team

Geriatric
Three goals scored by
Germans

Germanic
Mad virus

Germinate
Klaus is full

Germination
A very unhealthy
country

fig.141 Geranium

Ghost
Expression of astonishment in an Indian restaurant

Ghoulish
Hungarian stew that comes back to haunt you

Geranium – Glamorgan

Giblets
Tiny little scaffolds

Giggle
Very small music event

Gigolo
Jennifer Lopez running

Gingivitis
Compulsive dancing in red-heads

Glade
A ventriloquist's knife

Gladiator
Unrepentant cannibal

Glamorgan
Male version of the vajazzle

fig.142 Giblets

Gg

Gloating
Jamaican lightbulb

Global
Male bovine near Sellafield

Globular
An overweight vampire

Gnu
Opposite of g-old

fig. 143 Globular

Goatherd
Exclamation while flushing

Goblet
A small mouth

Gondolier
Something you catch from a boatman

Gonorrhea
Behind with the rent

fig. 144 Goblet

Gooseberry
A big duck's hat

Granary
An old folk's home

Grandee
Jack's grandmother

Grandiloquent
Naughty old lady

Grandstand
Granny's been to the solarium

fig.145 Gooseberry

Granite
Game of tag played in an old folk's home

Granule
Father Christmas's mother

Grasshopper
Useless lawn mower

Gg

Grating
Jamaican elephant

Grave digger
Serious enthusiast

Gravy
Close to death

fig.146 Gravy

Gregorian
Either of the Chappell brothers

Gringo
Mexican traffic lights

Gripe
What Australians make wine from

Groin
The 'go' light in Birmingham

Grumbling appendix
The space at the back of a book for complaints

Guacamole
A Mexican visitor to Toad Hall

Guitar
A grumpy old pirate

Gurgle
To steal a ventriloquist's dummy

Gyroscope
A device for locating dole money

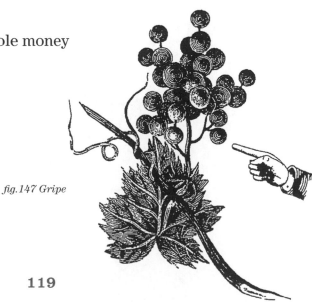

fig.147 Gripe

Hh

fig.148 Hobgoblin

Hacksaw
A tabloid report

Haddock
An enclosure for sea horses

Haemorrhage
A line of piles

Hagiology
The study of old bags

Haiku
Pigeon on helium

Hailstone
Formal greeting to Sir Mick Jagger

Hairspray
Incontinent German

fig.149 Haddock

Hh

Hairy
A bit like a German

Halitosis
Smelly comet

Hamas
What Geordies use to bang nails in

Hammer
Vincent Price

Hamstring
Sexy underwear for a pig

Haphazard
Mind the hap!

Harlequin
One of a set of five motor-bikes

fig. 150 Halitosis

fig. 151 Haphazard

Hairy – Haute cuisine

Harlot
A pirate

Harmony
Cash paid to comedians

Harpist
Fairly drunk

Harpoon
Scottish bragging

fig.152 Harpist

Harvest
What you wear under a harshirt

Hat-trick
A pile of freshly mown hats

Haute cuisine
Porridge

fig.153 Hat-trick

Hh

Haywain
Essex greeting

Headwind
A burp

Heathrow
What a baggage handler does

Heave ho
Laughing till you're sick

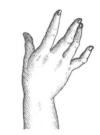

Hebrew
Jewish teabag

Hedgerow
Hedgehog eggs

fig.154 Hiding

Hee-haw
A male prostitute

Henceforward
Poultry advancing

Henna
Like a hen but even more so

Herbicide
The murder of a Volkswagen Beetle

fig.155 Herbicide

Heresy
A Vatican pop group

Herpes
What my wife wins prizes for at the local flower show

Hiding
A bell you can't reach

fig.156 Henceforward

Hh

Himalaya
Hermaphrodite chicken

Hindsight
Builder's cleavage

Hippocampus
Large African mammals at Butlins

Hirsute
Ladies' clothing

Hispanic
Fear of snakes

fig.157 Himalaya

fig.158 Hirsute

Hither
A snake with a hair lip

Hittite
What Princess Anne will do if you get her riled

Hoarding
A prostitute's microwave

Hobgoblin
1. Eating stoves
2. Antony Worrall Thompson

Hobnob
Cooking accident

Hobnobbing
Casual sex with a goblin

fig.159 Hobnob

Hh

Hoedown
Agricultural strike

Hogmanay
Someone who may be considered to have too large a collection of a particular impressionist painter

Hollyhock
Cheap Christmas wine

Hologram
Disappointing birthday stripper

Homophobe
Somebody who doesn't like *The Simpsons*

Homophobic
Allergic to Greek epic poetry

Homophone
Gay chat line

fig.160 Hopscotch

Homosexual
Randy *Simpsons* fan

Honolulu
To give an MBE to a Scottish singer

Hootenanny
A goat with a big nose

Hopscotch
One-legged Glaswegian

Hormone
Professional fake orgasm

Hornby
A sexy bee

fig.161 Homophobic

Hh

Horology
The study of prostitutes

Horseshoe
Cross between a stallion and a sheep

Horticulture
Grand opera

Hosanna
A loose girl's name

Hosepipe
A dance by sailors
wearing tights

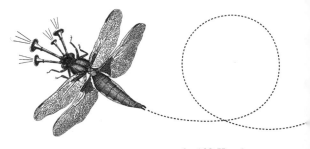

fig.162 Humbug

Hospice
Equestrian discharge

Hospital
Prostitute's lubricant

Hotpot
Stolen drugs

Horology – Humphrey

Huggermugger
One step up from Hug a Hoodie

Hullabaloo
How to greet a bear

Humanitarian
Someone who only eats people

Humbug
Musical insect

Humdinger
A fly swat

Humphrey
A good sound system

fig.163 Hullabaloo

Hh

Humpty Dumpty
One who is humped and dumped

Hundred
Fear of Germans

Hunky-dory
A butch fish

Hurdy gurdy
Opposite of 'his digurdy'

Hurricane
A riding crop

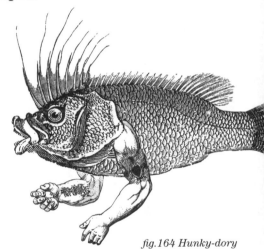
fig.164 Hunky-dory

Hutzpa
Character in Shakespeare's *Henry V*

Hyacinth
Elevated keyboard

Hydrangea
Warning from Tonto

Humpty Dumpty – Hysteria

Hydrant
An ant with three heads

Hydraulics
To conceal the things that you rest your oars in

Hypocrite
Hippopotamus review

Hypotenuse
The upstairs lavatory's engaged

Hysteria
Climbing plant that makes you laugh

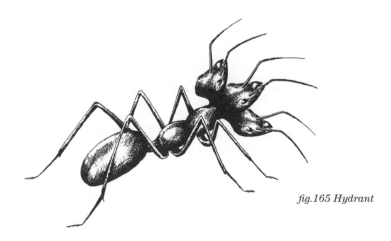

fig.165 Hydrant

fig.166 Iconoclastic

I Claudius
Digital emperor

Icelander
To tell lies about Apple

Icicle
A small bike made by Apple

Icicles
What an Eskimo has between his legs

Icon
Optical illusion

Iconoclastic
A rubber band for securing religious paintings

Iconography
Filthy Byzantine pictures

fig.167 Icicle

Ii

Idiomatic
Foolproof dish washer

Igloo
Digital adhesive

Ignoramus
Someone who is both stupid
and an arse

Iguana
Inuit dwelling made of bird poo

Imitate
Pretend to be an art gallery

Impact
Pixie stand-up

fig.168 Imitate

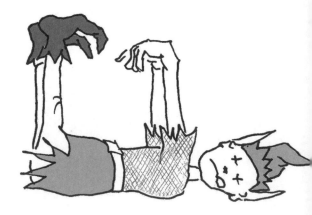

fig.169 Impending

Idiomatic – Impolite

Impair
The stuff that gets cut at a pixie barber's

Impart
Pixie painting

Impeccable
Bird proof

Impending
Death of a pixie

Implication
An ointment for little pixies

Implode
Heavy luggage carried by a pixie

Imply
Untruth told by a pixie

Impolite
A pixie on fire

fig.170 Impeccable

Ii

Import
What posh pixies drink after dinner

Important
The immigrant ant that the depressant doesn't like

Importune
Jeremy Hardy

In denial
Where some
Egyptians wash
their clothes

Inadvertent
Sponsored
camping

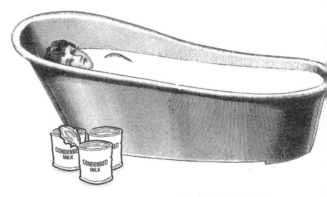

fig.171 Incarnation

Incarnation
Immersed in condensed milk

Incessant
An ant that's sleeping with its sister

Incidental
False teeth overboard!

Income
Entrance

Increment
The opposite of excrement

Incumbent
MPs' expenses

Indelible
A bull in Delhi

Indict
When the Queen is unsure about something

fig.172 Indelible

Ii

Indiscernible
We preferred Eric

Indulgence
At a boring urinal

Industrialize
To write the words 'clean me' on the
back of someone's van

Ineffable
Something you can't swear
about

Infantile
Where they keep the children's
products in a supermarket

Infantry
A baby oak

fig.173 Infantry

Inferno
Don't wear mink

Inflate
Her Majesty's plane has taken off

Inhabit
Dressed as a monk

Injury
Late singer of The Blockheads

Innuendo
An Italian suppository

Insane
Where some Parisians wash their clothes

fig.174 Inhabit

Ii

Insolent
Having fallen off the Isle of Wight ferry

Institute
A freeze-dried hooker

Insurance
To take out a policy on your ant farm

Insurgent
A washing powder for terrorists

Integrate
Answer to the question 'where's t' coal?'

Integrates
A fireplace enthusiast

Intelligence
Urinal with a micro-processor

fig.175 Integrates

Intense
Camping

Intent
Determination to go camping

Intercede
Keen gardener

Intercontinental
A person who has wet himself all
over the world

Interface
A sad expression put on at burials

Interfere
Lover of horror movies

Interflora
Excited about margarine

Interlude
A mucky person

fig.176 Interface

Ii

Intermittent
Where I go when camping

Internet
Where England footballers fail to put the ball

Interred
The position Prime Ministers often finds themselves in

Intifada
A chain of West Bank florists

Intimate
Tim dined at home

Intrude
Yorkshire for polite

fig.177 iPod

Inverse
Rhyming

Invest
Bruce Willis

Investigate
Pensions scandal

Investment
Thermal underwear for bankers

Inviolate
Dressed in purple

iPod
Optical aid using peas

Ipswich
What you turn your hip on with

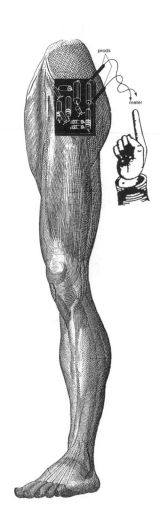

fig.178 Ipswich

Ii

Iris
Short Dubliner

Isometric
I so absolutely don't deal in yards, feet and inches

Isthmus
Yuletide in the years BC

Itching
Ancient Chinese book of dermatology

Ivy
Roman for 'four'

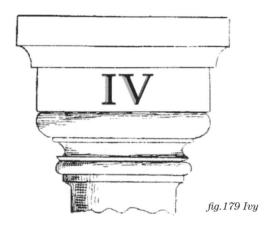

fig.179 Ivy

fig.180 Judicious

Jj

Jacobites
Michael Jackson's range of snacks

Jacuzzi
French for 'I know who did that in the bath'

Jasmine
Kenny Ball's band

Jigsaw
Chaffing that affects the cast of *Riverdance*

Jihad
The cry of the fundamentalist cowboy

Jocular
Scots vampire

Judgemental
Two weeks community service for armed robbery

fig.181 Jocular

Judicious
Hebrew crockery

Judo
Kosher plasticine

Jugular
A busty vampire

Jukebox
What Philip wears for cricket

Juniper
Did you bite that woman?

fig.182 Jukebox

fig.183 Jacuzzi

fig.184 Kirby grip

Ketchup – Kirby grip

fig.185 Kilocycle

Ketchup
To draw level

Khaki
A device for starting an automobile

Killjoy
Gloomy East Anglian antiques dealer

Kilocycle
A bike with no saddle

Kimono
Yoko's sister

Kindle
A state-of-the-art book that burns itself

King's Cross Station
A royal lobster

Kinship
A ship you're angry with

Kirby grip
North Yorkshire handshake

fig.186 King's Cross Station

Kk

Kit-Kat
Self-assembly feline

Kittiwake
Vigil for a dead cat

Knacker's yard
Enormous underpants

Knapsack
A sleeping bag

Knapweed
A damp sheet

Knee pads
Scottish turnip commercials

Knick-knack
An ability to steal

Knock-kneed
There's no doorbell

Kookaburra
Stove-on-Trent

fig.187 Knacker's yard

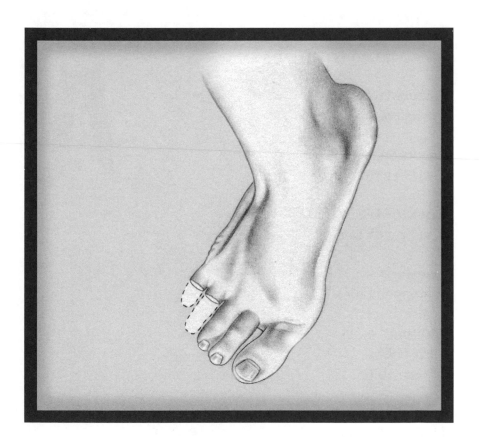

fig. 188 Lactose

Ll

Laburnum
A French barbecue

Laceration
Young woman's speech

Lackadaisical
Bicycle made for one

Lacklustre
The French bunch

Lactic
A stopped clock

Lactose
1. A pobble
2. Frostbite

Ladder
Like a lad, but even
more so

fig.189 Laburnum

fig.190 Lambada

Laburnum – Lamination

Laggard
A prison warder

Lamb shank
Sean Connery's sheep has drowned

Lambada
A sheep with no legs

Lambasted
Illegitimate sheep

Lamentable
Yorkshire for 'the Sunday
roast is ready'

Laminated
Pregnant sheep

Lamination
New Zealand

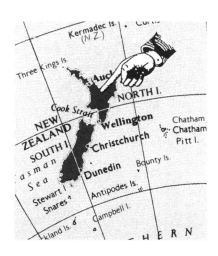

fig.191 Lamination

Ll

Lampoon
A device for whaling at night

Lancelot
A doctor during a boil epidemic

Languid
Laid-back Welsh village

Laplander
A clumsy private dancer

Larder
Chubbier than most

Largesse
A large 'S'

Lassitude
Bitten by a collie

fig.192 Largesse

fig.193 Leotard

Lampoon – Leprechaun

Latest
An entrance exam for prostitutes

Latex
The French CID

Laundress
Grass skirt

Lavish
A bit like a toilet

Legal
A sixteen-year-old bird of prey

Leicestershire
Why shearers like small sheep

Leotard
An idiot in lycra

Leprechaun
A variety of wheat whose ears fall off

fig.194 Laundress

Ll

Liability
Political skill

Libel
Australian price tag

Lieutenant
Person renting your toilet

Lightsabre
An old fluorescent tube

Likeness
Highlands enthusiast

Limpet
A little limp

Lip-sync
A lady's intimate wash basin

Liquorice
A bit like alcohol

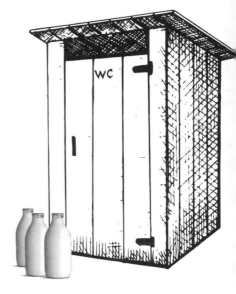

fig.195 Lieutenant

Listless
Upright

Literally
To drop rubbish in
a narrow passage

Liveable
Where Scousers
come from

Livelihood
An exuberant
gangster

Liverpool
Organ sharing scheme

Livery
Rather like liver

Loafer
An idle baker

fig.196 Likeness

fig.197 Livelihood

Ll

Loathing
An object on the bottom shelf

Lobster
A tennis player who favours
high, deep shots

Lockjaw
The correct emergency
procedure for disabling
Brian Blessed

Locomotion
A barely audible riot

Logarithm
Lumberjack on drums

Loggerheads
Lumberjack fanatics

Logical
A very small masonic meeting house

fig.198 Logarithm

Loathing – Loophole

Loiter
Device used by smokers in
the West Country

Londonderry air
Pippa Middleton

Longitude
He should have cut it up smaller

Loofah
An outdoor toilet

Looming
An antique porcelain lavatory

Loophole
A very long lavatory brush

fig.199 Looming

fig.200 Loophole

Ll

Lovelorn
To be very, very fond of grass

Ludo
Filthy version of Cluedo

Lupine
An air freshener

Lymph
To walk with a lisp

Lyricist
A complaint suffered by songwriters

fig.201 Lymph

fig.202 Melancholy

Mm

Macadam
A Scottish brothel-keeper

Macarena
Scottish stadium

Macaroni
Inventor of the pasta wireless

Macaroon
To leave a Scotsman on a desert island

fig.203 Macaroon

Mace
What the Queen puts traps down for

Macho
Inflammable stick used by smokers in Spain

Magenta
Here comes the Queen

fig.204 Maisonette

Maisonette
A tiny freemason

Majestic
A sceptre

Making
Husband of May queen

Maladjusted
Lazy duck

Malady
A bit like a duck

Malcontent
Someone who's perfectly
happy with Malcolm

Malfunction
A party in a shopping centre

Malcolm

fig.205 Malcontent

Mm

Malleable
Suitable for matrimony in China

Malteser
Coming soon: a shopping centre!

Manchester
A specialist in cosmetic surgery for ladyboys

Mange tout
Seconds please

Mangoes
He leaves

Manifesto
Jewish conjuror

Manifold
Origami

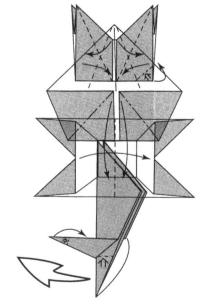

fig.206 Manifold

Manoeuvre
Unused vacuum cleaner

Margate
The mother of all scandals

Mariachi
What you do when you've been
engaged to Archie

Marigold
Get rich quick

Marinade
A soft drink for weddings

fig.207 Maritime

Marionette
What you do when you've been engaged to Annette

Maritime
When the wedding starts

Mm

Marmalade
The cry of a new-born chick

Marmite
An insect found on mothers

Marooned
The state you're in after falling into a vat of plums

Martini
A very small supermarket

Mascot
Somewhere to sleep
during a church service

Massachusetts
A large collection of
dentures

Masseuse
A roomful of stutterers

Masticate
To enjoy yourself with a
set of dentures

fig.208 Marmite

Mastication
Sealant abuse

Mastiff
  1. A row during a church service
  2. Boys at a Britney Spears concert

Matador
Preparing the front of your house for muddy shoes

Maternity
Yorkshire for 'it's my go at golf'

Matricide
The danger of smoking in bed

Mattress
A female mat

Mayfly
A Virgin plane

Maypole
Possibly Polish

fig.209 Mastiff

Mm

Meander
She and I

Measles
What artists use for self-portraits

Media
Tasting more strongly of mead

Megahertz
Extremely painful

Megawatt
PARDON!?

Melancholy
Funny-shaped dog

Membership
Amusingly-shaped boat

Memory stick
Amnesia

fig.210 Meander

Memsahib
The same Swedish car

Menacing
A male voice choir

Mendacity
Urban renewal programme

fig.211 Mendips

Mendips
Cannibal buffet

Menstrual
Medieval musician who performs once a month

Merciful
Liverpool's flooded

Merseyside
Killing of Scousers

fig.212 Measles

Mm

Metaphorical
Encountered a lady for
a short time

Metatarsals
Got together at Jeffrey
Archer's

Methane
How Macbeth introduces himself

Metronome
A dwarf on the Paris underground

Miasma
The reason I have an inhaler

Mice
What the Queen says when she means one mouse

Microbe
A tiny little dressing gown

fig.213 Methane

Metaphorical – Minimal

Microbiology
The study of shopping cheaply

Microfiche
Sardines

Midwifery
Part-way through breaking wind

Migraine
That corn doesn't belong to you

Militate
A tiny little art gallery

Mingling
A junior minger

Minimal
Small shopping centre

fig.214 Microfiche

Midwif

fig.215 Midwifery

Mm

Minion
A tiny shallot

Ministrate
Junior magistrate

Minsk
Camp Russian walk

Minuscule
Toddlers' playgroup in Liverpool

Mirth
A French moth

Mischief
Head girl

Miscomprehension
Winner of the English Grammar Beauty Contest

fig.216 Minsk

fig.217 Misprint

Misfit
A great-looking teacher

Mishmash
What Sean Connery will do if
he doesn't get to church on
Sunday

Misplace
Seafood beauty contest winner

fig.218 Missile

Misprint
To run in the wrong direction

Missile
   [1] An air stewardess
   [2] Where they keep the feminine products
       in a supermarket

Missing
A lady who is obsessed with gerunds

Mississippi
Wife of Mister Ippi

Mm

Missive
South African for 'very big'

Mistake
Winner of a butcher's beauty contest

Misty
To forgo the 4pm meal

Mitigate
A fantasy scandal

Mitosis
What's on the end of my feetsis

Mobster
An aggressive crustacean

Module
Christmas with The Who

Mogadon
My cat's a professor

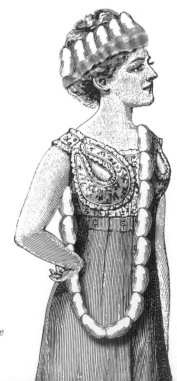

fig.219 Mistake

Missive – Moreover

Molten lava
Maggot shedding its winter coat

Monkey
Rather like a monk

Monochrome
A bath with only one tap

Monogamy
Celebrating New Year in
Scotland by yourself

fig.220 Mogadon

Moonlit
Collective term for fashionable novels about the moon

Morass
Having put on weight

Morbid
Unhealthily addicted to auctions

Moreover
An overweight dog

fig.221 Moreover

Mm

Morrissey
A bit like a Morris Dancer

Mortar
The difference between Marlboro
Reds and Marlboro Lights

Mosquito
A tiny place of Muslim worship

Motorist
A painful condition affecting drivers

Motorway
Device for removing those ditches
around castles

Mountaineer
Task for a very specialized taxidermist

Mountebank
Careless driving

fig.222 Mountaineer

Morrissey – Mushrooms

Moustache
Got to run

Mucus
A foul-mouthed cat

Multiple
To heat wine

Mumble
Unwanted mother you take to a secondhand shop

Mumps
Heaps of unwanted mothers

Muscatel
Smelly guest house

Mushrooms
What Lawrence
Llewelyn-Bowen does

F**K!

BOLL**KS!

A*SE!

fig.223 Mucus

Mm

Mutant
Cross between a cat
and an insect

fig.224 Mutant

Mutate
An art gallery for cats

Mutineer
Deaf mystic

Myspace
A hole in the skirting board

Mystery
A bit like a man

Mystical
The daughter of Mr Tickle

Myth
A female moth

fig.225 Myth

fig.226 Negligent

Nn

Nanometer
A device for counting grannies

Nanotechnology
The wife of Grandad o'Technology

Natterjack
A telephone socket

fig.227 Natterjack

Navigate
Scandal concerning road diggers

Navigator
A crocodile that knows where it's going

Neath
Things found in the middle of your legth

Nectarine
 1. To swallow a huge bowl of soup in one go
 2. Giraffe pâté

Nanometer – Neutered

Negligent
Man who wears
lingerie

Neighbourhood
The gangster next
door

Nematode
An avenging frog

Neologism
Prehistoric ejaculate

Nescafé
A loch-side diner

Netherlands
Falls on her bottom

Neutered
I've just been to the
lavatory

fig.228 Netherlands

fig.229 Nematode

Nn

New Delhi
Eleanor gets her kit off

Newcastle
To drop a hydrogen bomb on Piers
Morgan

Nicaragua
Underwear for big cats

Niceties
Pleasant sofas

Nicorette
Skimpy briefs

Nicotine
To arrest a youth

Nobleman
Eunuch

Noblesse
Somebody who didn't meet the Pope on his recent visit

fig.230 Non dom

Noblesse oblige
Someone who's quite happy that they didn't meet the Pope on his recent visit

Nodule
Pistols at dawn is cancelled

Noisette
A small noise

Nomination
A country where they love their food

Non dom
A defective contraceptive

Nonchalant
Double booked at Butlins

Norfolk
Disappointing night out in Yorkshire

fig.231 Nicotine

Nn

Norway
A Geordie expression
of surprise

Nosedive
Bad plastic surgery

Notable
You'll have to have your
dinner on the floor

Nurture
A Chas 'n' Dave song

Nutcase
A hat

Nutcrackers
Tight Y-fronts

Nutmeg
To assault the star
of *When Harry Met
Sally*

fig.232 Nosedive

fig.233 Notable

fig.234 Osmosis

Oo

O'clock
An Irish clock

Oatmeal
Three courses of haute cuisine

Obeisance
Irish washbowls

Obesity
Dallas

Obituary
Irish spitefulness

Oblique
Irish for desolate

fig.235 Offset

Oboe
 [1.] American tramp
 [2.] Irish device for shooting arrows

Obscenity
VD tips

Occupants
Underwear for squatters

Odin
Irish noise

Offence
Irish railing

Offend
To circumcise

Officious
Irish cod

Offset
The regulatory body that inspects badgers

fig.236 Occupants

Oo

Omelette
A small Buddhist

Omit
An Irish glove

Onesie
What the Queen calls a selfie

Online
Traditional method of drying washing

Onomatopoeia
The first sign of a weak bladder

Onus
A very round bottom

Opening
Irish writing

Optical
To giggle during surgery

fig.237 Onus

Optimist
The view through a cataract

Orchestral
Alternative bird of prey

Orchid
The son of a Brummie

fig.238 Omelette

Organ donor
A sub-standard kebab

Organism
An irrational prejudice against Wurlitzers

Orienteering
Court case in Japan

Orinoco
A citrus fruit flavoured chocolate beverage

Oo

Orthodontist
Those very devout dentists with the beards and the hats

Oscillate
Dame Edna hasn't turned up

Osmosis
Early Australian prophet

Ostracise
About as big as an ostrich

Otter
Nice weather in Yorkshire

Outrank
To be smellier than

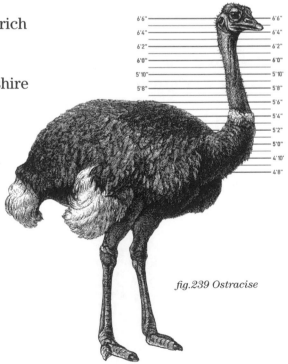

fig.239 Ostracise

Ovaltine
A fat adolescent

Overabundance
To waltz round a small
bread roll on the ground

Overrate
Nine

Overture
Bridge on Yorkshire river

fig.240 Orthodontist

Ovulation
When the audience stand and throw eggs

Oxymoron
Stupid cow

Oyster
Someone who sprinkles his conversation with Yiddish
expressions

fig.241 Pandemonium

Paddy field
Irish cricketer

Padlocks
An Irish wig

Painful
Complete with windows

Paint
Vulgar version of 'pisn't'

Paintings
Jamaican paracetamol

Palaver
Complicated knitting pattern

Palisade
What the Queen drinks

Palmistry
Not knowing who your dad is

fig.242 Palisade

Pp

Palpitation
Indian preacher

Paltry
A skinny chicken

Pancreas
A gland located next to King's Cross

Pandemonium
A black and white musical instrument that won't breed in captivity

Pantaloon
Underwear fetishist

Panting
Jamaican cooking receptacle

Pantomime
Underwear for the hard of hearing

fig.243 Pantry

Pantry
What pants grow on

Papal
The Vatican system for
donating online

Paper cut
Payment system for barbers

fig.244 Paradox

Parabolic
The effect of a too-tight parachute harness

Parachute
Exit for troopers leaving the barracks

Paradox
Flying doctors

Paraffin
Flying fish

Parallax
Laxative for a parrot

fig.245 Paraffin

Pp

Paramount
An over-attentive soldier

Paranoia
1. A fear of people dropping out of the sky
2. Dad gets on your nerves

Paranoid
An angry person who jumps out
of aeroplanes

Parapet
An airborne cat

fig.246 Parapet

Paraquat
A species of parrot that nobody likes

Parasites
Views from the Eiffel Tower

Parental
Dads for hire

fig.247 Parental

Paramount – Particular

Parenthood
Split condom

Parkour
Prostitute who hangs round
municipal gardens

Parsimonious
Indian singer

Parsley
A bit like a parcel

Parsnip
Dad's vasectomy

Participation
When your dad joins in

Particles
Ma's taken her feather
duster to him again

Particular
Fun-loving vampire

fig.248 Parsnip

fig.249 Particular

Pp

Passport
Father's race

Pasta
Italian priest

Pasteurize
Right inside your head

fig.250 Pastiche

Pastiche
What Sean Connery eats in Cornwall

Pastoral
Too old for foreplay

Pastrami
The art of meat folding

Paterfamilias
Well-known comedy routine

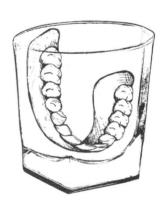

fig.251 Pastoral

Peanuts
Far worse than kidney stones

Pear tree
What posh poets like to write

Peccadillo
An armour-plated condom

Peckish
Rather like Gregory Peck

Pedicure
Medicine for children

Peewit
A funny piss artist

Peking duck
Evasive action taken by voyeur when
fearing detection

fig.252 Peccadillo

Pp

Pending
The noise a novelty writing instrument makes

Pendulous
When you can put a pen under it and it stays there

Pendulum
Storage room for biros

Penitent
Canvas condom

Pensive
Something you can write with
while draining the potatoes

Pentagram
Occult stripper

fig.253 Pending

Pentecost
The price of posh ladies' knickers

Pending – Permeate

Peperami
What Sergeant Pepper served in

Pepper pot
A pot belonging to one who stutters

Percussion
How Scottish soft furnishers are paid

Perfect
The cat's pregnant

Perforce
Cat's army

Peripatetic
A disappointing chilli sauce

Permeate
A curly-haired rowing crew

fig.254 Pentagram

fig.255 Perfect

Pp

Permit
Cat skin glove

Permutation
The theory of how hairdos evolved

Perpetuate
How Korean restaurants get paid

Persecute
Dandy dick

Persist
Rate set by doctors for removing growths

Perspire
How a steeplejack gets
paid

Perth
Where Chris Eubank
keeps his cash

fig.256 Permit

fig.257 Persist

Pervade
Financial help for deviants

Perverse
How poets get paid

Perversion
The cat's side of the story

Pesto
Athlete's foot

Petal
Newcastle gasoline

Petulance
A vehicle that takes dogs and cats to hospital

Petulant
The ant who sang 'Downtown'

fig.258 Petulance

Pp

Pharmacist
Old Macdonald had a boil

Pheromones
Tutankhamun's complaints

Philander
The Duke of Edinburgh and the Queen

Philanthropist
A kindly drunk

Philharmonic
To feed the Queen

Phlegmatic
Battery-powered
handkerchief

fig.259 Phlegmatic

Physiology
The study of lemonade

Physique
A Perrier enema

Piano
A musical shipping line

Picador
Find your own way out

Piccaninny
An election

Pie crust
What you get if you don't polish your pike

Piece-meal
Dinner after a row

fig.260 Physiology

Pp

Pigsticking
Clockwork pork

Pile
Australian bucket

Pilgrim
Depressive drug

fig.261 Pigsticking

Pillage
A pharmaceutically dependent village

Pillock
A small stupid hill

Pillory
Chemist

Pillow
Suppository too big?

fig.262 Pile

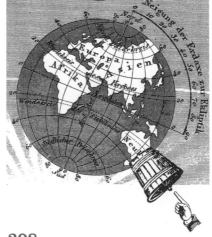

Pinafore
A system of signalling at sea with aprons

Pinnacle
The humane slaughter of kitchen aprons

Pinprick
Not well endowed

Piper
What Australians write on

Pistachio
Facial hair grown while drunk

Pistol
Entry fee for coin-operated public toilet

Piston
Taken advantage of

fig.263 Pinafore

Pp

Pith helmet
Thorry, it wath an emergenthy

Pitter-patter
Someone who slaps Greek bread

Pity
A bit like a pit

Pixelate
An over-due elf

Placate
To calm an actress by offering her a role in a Winslet biopic

Placebo
The Marx Brother who was fired because people only *thought* he was good

Placenta
Spanish kindergarten

fig.264 Pith helmet

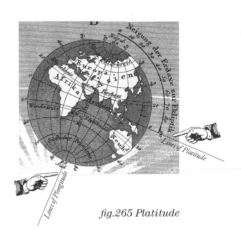

fig.265 Platitude

Plainsong
'Y Viva España' on landing

Plaintiff
A row with a stewardess

Plantation
Bad police practice

Platitude
   1. So hungry he ate the plate
   2. The opposite of 'plongitude'

Platypus
To give your cat pigtails

Plebiscite
Web page for common people

fig.266 Platypus

Plinth
Artist formerly known as having two
speech defects

Plonker
Drinker of cheap wine

Pp

Plutocrat
Someone who votes for
a Disney character

PMT
Afternoon
refreshment

fig.267 PMT

Podcast
To fish with peas

Pointless
To reduce the amount of times
you gesture with your finger

Pokemon
Jamaican proctologist

Polaroids
Inflammation caused by sitting on icebergs

Poldark
To canvass someone during a power cut

Police
Chamber pot rental

Polish
What not to call the police after a few drinks as you get into your car

Politician
A parrot named after a painter

Poltroon
Parrot from Scotland

Polygamist
Two-timing parrot

Polygamy
The ancient art of wife-folding

Polymath
Numerate parrot

fig.268 Poltroon

Pp

Polynesia
Forgetting lots of things

Polypropylene
That parrot's terribly thin

Polyunsaturated
A dry parrot

Pomegranate
Australian expression used to describe English stone

Pom-pom
Australian word for English twins

Ponderous
Shop that sells ponds

fig.269 Pom-pom

fig.270 Ponderous

Polynesia – Porpoise

Pontefract
To theorise about Yorkshire

Pontificate
A lecture on French bridges

Poplar
A tree everybody likes

Poppadom
A contraceptive made from bubble wrap

Poppycock
A streaker on November 11th

Porcupine
A reluctant vegetarian

Porpoise
Dolphin on a mission

fig.271 Poppycock

fig.272 Pontificate

Pp

Porsche
Really, really posh

Portal
To offer Mr Capone an after-dinner drink

Portent
A leaky marquee

Portly
Shaped like a harbour

Post modern
Emails

Posterity
Inherited bottom size

Posthumous
The act of delivering Greek food by mail

fig.273 Postulate

Postmistress
Sex by correspondence course

Postulate
New name for Royal Mail

Potent
A camping convenience

Potpourri
Aroma of dried Telly Tubby

Poultry
A small amount of chickens

Preach
Soft fruit with a speech defect

Preamble
To get ready for a walk

fig.274 Potpourri

Pp

Precipice
Push-button toilet

Precipitate
An art gallery on a cliff

Precursor
One who swears in advance

Prehensile
An island formerly occupied by chickens

Pre-Raphaelite
One who leaves before the raffle

Pretence
The days before camping

Pretext
Letters and phone calls

Primark
A first coat of paint applied by Noah

fig.275 Precipitate

Precipice – Proficiency

Primula
A rather prudish vampire

Privilege
An outdoor loo on the tenth floor

Problematic
Dodgy loft conversion

Proboscis
Against the workers

Prodigal
To poke a seabird

Produce
In favour of squash

Proficiency
In favour of salt-water wildlife

fig.276 Prodigal

fig.277 Primula

Pp

Profiteering
Controversial item of jewellery
in the shape of Mohammed

Profundity
In favour of a comic song

Programme
I so absolutely don't do stones, pounds and ounces

Prolapse
In favour of having your dinner in front of the telly

Proletarian
Someone who only eats common people

Propaganda
A good look

Propagate
Rather respectable scandal

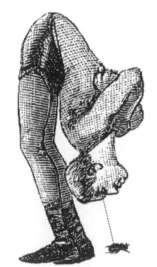

fig.278 Propaganda

Propane
People who are into S&M

Property
A decent cuppa

Prophylactic
Holder of the Chair in milk

Prosaic
Written by someone on antidepressants

Prosthetic
Not a very good call girl

Protests
Call-girl exams

Psychedelia
Mental cook

fig.279 Property

Pp

Psychiatric
Guessing right three times in a row

Psychological
Something that makes sense on a bil

Psychopath
Crazy paving

Pubescent
Intimate deodorant

fig.280 Psychological

Pulpit
  1. Warren Beatty's bed
  2. What to do with a Jeffrey Archer novel

Pumpkin
Have sex with relatives

Punish
Rather like a pun

fig.281 Purlieu

Punjab
To hit someone for a play on words

Punnet
A net for catching puns

Punster
What you must do to the mixture
to get a nice light currant pun

Puppetry
Little dogs' toilet

Purgatory
To slip Ex-lax into Michael Gove's coffee

Purlieu
Cross between an oyster and a sheep

fig.282 Puppetry

Pp

Push
What Sean Connery calls his cat

Pustule
Festive boil

Putin
Inexpensive bed pan

Pyrenees
Halfway up the pyralegs

Pyromaniac
One who collects glass
baking dishes

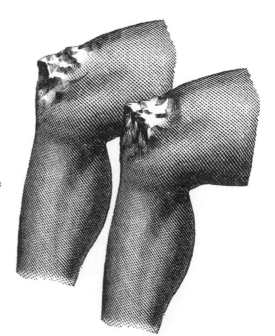

fig.283 Pyrenees

fig.284 Quaker

Qq

Quadrant
Four people shouting

Quaint
Vulgar version of 'quisn't'

Quaker
Posh duck

Quartermaster
25% schoolteacher

Quash
Quince cordial

Quatracento
Person who has seen Suzi
Quatro a hundred times

Quest
The Jonathan Ross family
coat of arms

Queue
An unencumbered
cucumber

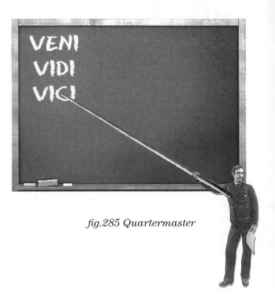

fig.285 Quartermaster

fig.286 Quicksilver

Quadrant – Quisling

Quick
Noise made by a New Zealand duck

Quicksilver
A pirate on a motorbike

Quietude
Ate one's food with one's mouth shut

Quince
Not quite a coincidence

Quisling
Underdeveloped question and answer

fig.287 Quadrant

fig.288 Rugged

Rabid
A bunny with a cold

Racism
Irrational hatred of a breakdown recovery service

Radar
An attack by pirates

Raffia
Craft fair organised crime syndicate

Ram raider
Dodgy vet

Rambling
Jewellery for sheep

fig.289 Rambling

Rr

Rampart
Essential element in
sheep breeding

Ramsgate
Farming scandal

Ramshackle
Male chastity belt

Randomize
A squint

Ransack
The act of making someone
redundant in a hurry

fig.290 Rampart

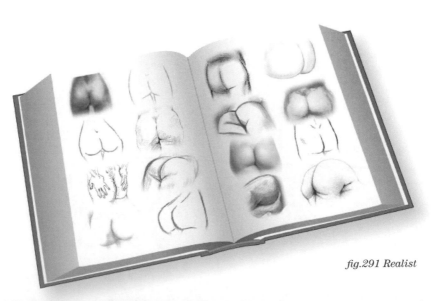

fig.291 Realist

Ransom
Half-hearted jog

Rapscallion
Funky spring onion

Ratatouille
The sound made by a
machine-gun ricochet

Ratchet
Rodent droppings

Razor
A lift

Reading
To ring a bell again

Realist
Catalogue of bottoms

fig.292 Randomize

Rr

Rebut
To have one's bottom lifted

Rebuttal
A bottom transplant

Receipt
To sit down again

Receptacle
Playful welcome from the lady at
the front desk

Recommend
To destroy it or fix it?

Recordable
Sash windows you can fix

Rectitude
The angle at which a thermometer
should be inserted

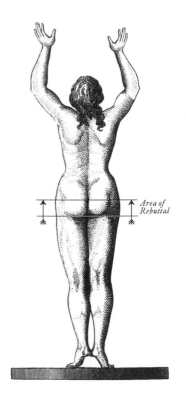

*Area of
Rebuttal*

fig.293 Rebut

Rectum
Indigestion

Recursive
Continually swearing

Referendum
Suppository for match officials

Regarding
Replacement security staff

Reiki
A bit like a rake

Reincarnation
Born again as a tin of
condensed milk

Reindeer
Polite weather forecast

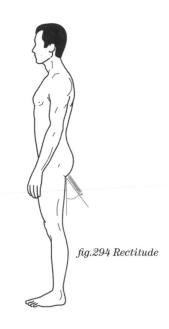

fig.294 Rectitude

fig.295 Reincarnation

Rr

Relenting
Giving up trying to give up Lent

Relief
What trees do in Spring

Remember
To join an organisation you left some time ago

Renegade
Device for blowing up anagram enthusiasts

Renewed
Undressed again

Renovate
To restore a French car

fig.296 Renovate

Repartee
To go out two nights in a row

Repercussion
Concerning that drummer

Replica
Someone who sucks up to the woman from Thomas Cook

Repository
Warehouse with delivery at the back

Reproach
To harvest fish

Republican
To get a new inn-keeper

Resource
To get more ketchup

fig.297 Reproach

Rr

Resuscitation
That monkey's from the Far East

Retail
Yorkshire bitter

Retard
Very difficult in Yorkshire

Retirement
Replacing the wheels on a car

Retread
Very red in Yorkshire

Rev counter
Survey of vicars

fig.298 Rev counter

Rev limiter
A bouncer at the local church

Revelation
Joy experienced when the car starts

Revenue
A vicar I once had the acquaintance of

Reversal
Dry run for a church service

Reverse
To rewrite part of a poem

Revolt
To charge a battery

Rheumatic
A loft conversion

fig.299 Rheumatic

Rr

Rind
What the Queen buys in a pub

Robot
An occupational disease of oarsmen

Robust
A broken oar

Roman nose
What Caesar used to wash his chariot

Rotterdam
Construction to prevent the
flow of Terry Thomas

Roulette
   1. A queen
   2. A tiny law

Routine
An adolescent kangaroo

Rubicon
Imitation gemstone

fig.300 Roman nose

Rugged
Wearing a wig

Rugger
A wig-maker

Rumania
A worrying over-fondness for kangaroos

Rum baba
A very strange sheep

Rumination
Under-populated country

Rusk
World domination board
game for babies

fig.301 Rugger

S s

fig.302 Sealant

Saab
Indian for 'Nice car, sir'

Sacrilegious
Bag worship

Sago
A good way to start a race

Samovar
Term describing how
many and whose planes
are missing

Sanctity
  [1.] Drooping bosom
  [2.] Multiple-breasted
     Frenchwoman

Sandy
That's convenient

Satellite
Burning behind

fig.303 Sacrilegious

Ss

Satire
Seated in a more elevated position

Satsuma
Japanese wrestling while sitting down

Saucier
Pain and redness in the eye

Saveloy
Hotel for sausages

Saxophone
Hotline to a salt supplier

Scampi
Fraudulent urine san

fig.304 Satire

Level of Satire

Satire – Scooby Doo

Scandals
Sandals with socks

Scar tissue
Problem attaching a DVD
player to the television

Scarf
To eat in Knightsbridge

fig.305 Scandals

Scarface
An accomplished knitter

Scatological
An intelligent jazz riff

Scintillate
To commit adultery till breakfast

Scooby Doo
A responsible dog owner

fig.306 Scarface

Ss

Scrap
It's rubbish

Scrapyard
I want metre

Scrumpy
To relieve oneself during the rugby

fig.307 Scurrilous

Scruple
Cross between a screw top and a ring pull

Scrutineer
What MFI tells you to do

Scum
It has arrived

Scurrilous
A mouse with no legs

fig.308 Sea lion

Scrap – Seesaw

Sea lion
An implement for
pressing seals

Sealant
Amphibious insect

fig.309 Sea-legs

Sea-legs
The eggs of the seal

Secretariat
Headwear for typists

Secular
How the Queen describes her wheels

Sedate
Meant nine

Seesaw
What Moses might have used
to part the Red Sea

fig.310 Seesaw

Ss

Selfish
What a fishmonger does

Semolina
A system of signalling with puddings

Senile
What to do in Egypt

Sentiment
The perfume he intended to buy

Sequencer
A sparkly knight

Serial killer
Combine harvester

Serviette
A bloke from communist Russia

fig.311 Semolina

fig.312 Serial killer

Servile
A nasty knight

Sewage
Legal work

Sex
What the Queen keeps her
coal in

Shack
What Sean Connery keeps
his coal in

Shagpile
An experience both painful
and pleasant

Shallot
No more onions

Shakespeare
Arab-owned seaside
amusement arcade

fig.313 Sequencer

Ss

Shambles
Imitation brambles

Shambling
Fake jewellery

Shambolic
False testicle

Shambolical
Padded Y-fronts

Shampoo
Fake dog turd

Shamrock
 1. Polystyrene boulder
 2. Tribute band

Shavings
What Sean Connery keeps in his bank account

Sheep dip
Unpopular buffet item

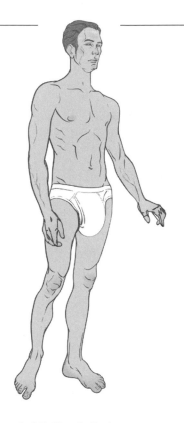

fig.314 Shambolical

Sheepish
Scottish for 'that girl is urinating'

Shellacking
Slug-like

Shellfish
A bit like a shelf

Shingle
Sean Connery's definition of a bachelor

Shinto
Leg diagram

Shire
Downpour in Gerrards Cross

Shit
What Sean Connery says to his dog

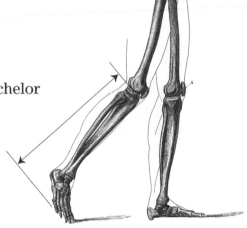

fig.315 Shinto

Ss

Shi-tzu
Disappointing animal
park

Shoddy
Big Ears' unkempt friend

Shoehorn
A fetish

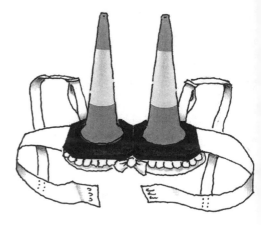

fig.316 Silicone

Shoot-out
Someone selling shoes
at above their market
value

Shrink wrap
A rubbish psychiatrist

Shrubbery
What Sean Connery says when he sends his
chicken back in a restaurant

Shuttlecock
A space chicken

Sidekick
A cowboy's friend who can tell the future

Signature
Baby swan droppings

Silicon
Stupid Tory

Silicone
Madonna's bra

Silicone hydrate
The percentage of actresses
pretending they haven't
had boob jobs

Singapore
Jeremy Hardy

fig.317 Shuttlecock

Ss

Ski lift
The elation you feel after
eating a yoghurt

Skid
A baby goat on ice

Skidoo
To slip on dog poo

Slapdash
Hit and run

Slight
It is dawn

Slippery
A bit like a slipper

Smelting
Jamaican for nose

fig.318 Skid

fig.319 Skidoo

Smirks
Geordie cigarettes

Snappy
What a baby crocodile wears

Snickers
Spanties

Snowball
Utterance from an umpire

Snowflakes
We've run out of cereal

Snuff box
Coffin

Soaring
That curry was too hot

fig.320 Snuff box

Ss

Sociopath
Serial killer who does wonders for your back pain

Solar
Precedes 'tee'

Solder
Military man with an eye missing

Somersault
Substance for de-icing the roads in July

Sometime
Maths lesson

Sorcerer
Even more of a saucer

Sorcery
A bit like a saucer

Sorcer   *Sorcerer*

fig.321 Sorcerer

Sorting
A Jamaican rash

Sou'wester
A pig with enormous teeth

Soulmate
Korean bride

fig.322 Sou'wester

Sounding-board
Yawning

Soupçon
Dinner's nearly ready

Soya milk
Looked in your fridge

Spain
What you experience when you've been spunched

Spatula
A single spat

Ss

Spatulate
An argument about punctuality

Specimen
Italian astronauts

Speckle
To spit at a stand-up comic

Spectacular
Short-sighted vampire

Spectate
A tiny little art gallery

Spectator
A short-sighted potato

Speculate
24-hour opticians

fig.323 Spectate

fig.324 Spectacular

Sperm donor
Worst kebab ever

Spermicide
The half of the bed you'd rather not sleep on

Spinach
Skin irritation caused by sitting too close to
Alastair Campbell

Splint
To run very fast with a broken leg

Splinter
Chinese 100-metre runner

Spokesman
A hippy admires a bike

Spokesperson
Cyclist

fig.325 Splint

Ss

Spoof
Person who is only pretending to be gay

Sporran
What Scottish frogs do in ponds

Sprouts
The opposite of sprints

Squeamish
A bit like a squeam

Stagnation
Scotland

Stalagmite
A tiny little prisoner of war

Star-struck
Nicole Kidman's lorry

fig.326 Spoof

fig.327 Stagnation

Statuette
What was it that you had for dinner?

Stencil
A very still pencil

Stereo
A long look from a Greek man

Stifle
A home for a pig designed along the lines of a Paris landmark

Stifling
A Scottish dance for pigs

Stipend
Pig house with a fence round it

Stockade
A charity for Oxo addicts

fig.328 Stifling

Ss

Stopcock
  1. A condom
  2. To become a lesbian

Stopgap
To campaign against competitively-priced denim

Stratosphere
Aftershave phobia

Strawberry
Grass hat

Stucco
Hitherto unknown Marx Brother

Stylist
Pig directory

Stymie
A Jewish pig

fig.329 Strawberry

fig.330 Stylist

Subdued
A less than cool person

Sublime
Underperforming citrus fruit

Subordination
Installing a priest underwater

Substantial
Not as good as the old Bonzo Dog Doo-Dah Band

Substitute
An underwater hooker

Subtext
To use a mobile under water

Suffix
Next to Kent

Suffocate
East Anglian postcode

fig.331 Subtext

Ss

Suffocation
A weekend in Lowestoft

Suffragette
Ryanair

Suggestive
A sexy biscuit

Suitable
A cow

Superficial
Steward in charge of the broth

Superglue
A really lovely Eskimo's house

fig.332 Supine

Supine
To take a tree to court

Suppository
Someone you've always suspected votes Conservative

Surcharge
What you pay for a knighthood

Surrogate
Stand-in Yorkshire spa town

Sweepstake
What Sooty cooks for dinner

Sycamore
Not as well as I used to be

Sycophants
When an anteater loses his appetite

Syllabus
Liverpool coach

fig.333 Sycophants

Ss

Symbolic
My mobile phone's on the blink

Symbols
Prosthetic testicles

Symmetry
A very neatly laid out graveyard

Syrupy
It might be a wig

Systematic
A robot nun

fig.334 Syrupy

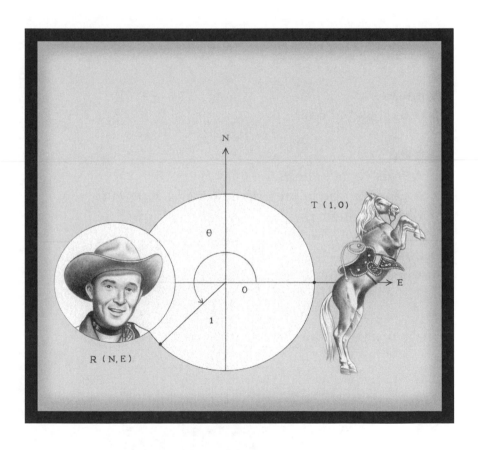

fig.335 Trigonometry

Tt

Tabby
A big church in Yorkshire

Tadpole
Ever so slightly Polish

Taffeta
 1. A Welsh goat's cheese
 2. A cannibal with a preference for Welsh people
 3. Diolch yn fawr

Tailback
Post-operative Manx cat

Tall
What's near the front door in Yorkshire

fig.336 Tailback

Tabby – Tanzanite

Tally-ho
A loose woman who keeps count

Tamper
What you take on a Yorkshire picnic

Tangent
Dale Winton

Tanker
What you use to moor a boat in
Yorkshire

fig.337 Tally-ho

Tannoy
To irritate loudly

Tantamount
To ride a French aunt

Tanzanite
What a beautician does to Sir Bob Geldof in Essex

fig.338 Tannoy

Tt

Tap
Yorkshire-based software
for t'iPhone

Tapas
To gently touch
someone's bottom

Tape
Yorkshire monkey

fig.339 Tape

Tapestry
Ornamental plumbing

Tapioca
A disappointingly average dance routine

Tardis
Request to council for repair of pothole

Tarmac
Scottish gratitude

Tart
What you'll see in a Yorkshire gallery

Tartar
Opposite of 'hello sailor'

Tatters
Where you buy hats in Yorkshire

Tax
Yorkshire hatchet

Teabag
Cha lady

Teetotal
Two on humans, four on cows

Telecommunication
Talking to the TV set

fig.340 Template

Telepathy
When you can't be bothered to turn over the TV

Template
The secretary hasn't turned up

Tt

Tena lady
Cheap date

Tendentious
Five pairs of false teeth

Tentacles
  1. Eyewear for campers
  2. Prehensile genitalia

Tentative
Not sure about camping

Tenure
How they describe a decade in the West Country

Tepee
Small tent outside a wigwam

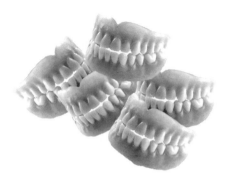

fig.341 Tendentious

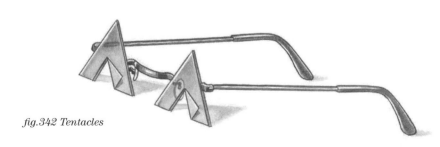

fig.342 Tentacles

Terminology
The study of Yorkshire fur

Terpsichorean
Kim Jong-un's
paintbrush cleaner

Terrain
Yorkshire bad
weather

Terrapin
Scary brooch

Terrorist
A Yorkshireman
prone to making
mistakes

fig.343 Tepee

Terse
What you see at a Yorkshire funeral

Testicle
A humorous question in an exam

Tt

Testicles
Experimental icicles

Testicular
A vampire who talks bollocks

Testimony
A lot of bollocks

Testosterone
Macho Italian soup

Tête-à-tête
To walk from one end of an art gallery to another

fig.344 Tetracycline

Tetracycline
Four on a bike

Teutonic
What you order with 'teugin'

Thatcher
Used to be married to that Sonny Bono

The Italian job
Taken short in Rome

Theatre Royal
Lubricant for auditoria

Thermidor
A Spanish lobster fighter

Thermos
The Greek god of picnics

fig.345 Thermidor

Tt

Thermostat
Body decoration showing the image of a flask

Thesaurus
Condition caused by eating the hot curry

Thespian
A woman who only sleeps with actresses

Thinking
A young Elvis

Thirst
The one before thecund

Threefold
This horse has had triplets

Throng
A three-piece thong

fig.346 Tiddlywinks

Tickertape
Temporary watch strap

Tiddlywinks
A nap after a good drink

Tie-dye
A neat Brummie

fig.347 Tickertape

Timbre
The cry of the French lumberjack

Tinker
An Irish philosopher

Tinsel
Gretel's more flamboyant other brother

Tint
Yorkshire word of disagreement

fig.348 Tinker

Tt

Tirade
A puncture call-out service

Tissues
Matters of importance in Yorkshire

Tit for tat
A French charity shop

Titillate
Delayed puberty

Titular
A vampire who no one thinks much of

Toadstool
Porn version of *The Wind in the Willows*

Toga
A dyslexic goat

fig.349 Tomahawk

Toil
What they use in Yorkshire to fry chips

Toilet
To rent out the children's playthings

Toils
What Brummies have on their roofs

Toll
What you try to put the ball in on a Yorkshire golf course

Tomahawk
A vegetable of prey

Tombola
Man who throws cats

Toothsome
To bite, but not everybody

fig.350 Toll

Tt

Topical
Branston's finest

Toronto
Expression used by the Lone Ranger
when drunkenly addressing his companion

Torpedo
A Glastonbury-based nonce

Torpid
Unfinished torpedo

Torquay
Geordie Christmas dinner

Torrid
Something horrible in Yorkshire

Torture
Rather like a torch but even more so

fig.351 Torpid

Toucans
A couple of tins

Towel rail
Where Yorkshire people keep their owls

Tracheotomy
The surgical removal of a shellsuit

Trail mix
To stalk Irishmen

Trainee
A bit like a train

fig.352 Towel rail

Tt

Tram
Male sheep in Yorkshire

Trampette
A lady tramp

Trampoline
Cleansing fluid for tramps

Transcendental
[1] Cross-dressing dentist (see also 'tooth fairy')
[2] To receive false teeth through the post from a drag act

Transgression
When female impersonators get cross

fig.353 Transistor

Transistor
A nun with surprisingly large hands

Translator
One who disparages cross-dressers

Transport
Cross-dressing athletes

Trapezoid
A circus robot

Trash
Yorkshire measles

Traumatize
Troubled neckware

Trench
Yorkshire spanner

Triangular
To test Mrs Merkel's patience

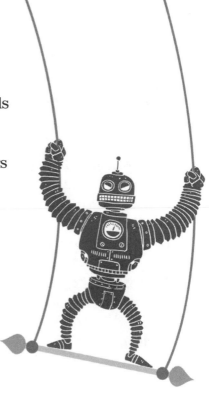

fig.354 Trapezoid

Tt

Tricycle
An even shorter trice

Trifle
  1. Three-barrelled shot-gun
  2. Yorkshire gun

fig.355 Trifle

Trifling
To attempt Scottish dancing

Trigonometry
A cowboy's mathematical method for locating his horse

Trilby
A bee that rings

Trinidad
Reply to the question: 'which of those two fashion experts do you fancy, son?'

fig.356 Trilby

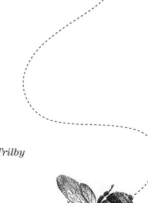

Tripod
  [1.] A carrier for tripe
  [2.] To prosecute peas

Trouble
Yorkshire building waste

Truculent
Your kind loan of a Transit

Trump
  [1.] Favourite Yorkshire steak
  [2.] Noxious blast of hot air from an arse

Trust
Iron erosion in Yorkshire

Tuba
Someone who makes tubes

fig.357 Tripod

Tt

Tumbling
A belly-button ring

Turbine
Windy headgear

Turd
Yorkshire cattle

Turkey
A bit like a Turk

Turmoil
Lubricant for use in school

Turpentine
A Geordie highwayman

Twee
What Yorkshire tea turns into

fig.358 Turbine

Tweet
Yorkshire grain

Twerk
What they do in Yorkshire between 9 and 5

Twiddle
Yorkshire term
cf. see under 'Twinkle'

Twig
Yorkshire toupée

Twiglets
Mr & Mrs Pinocchio's two
children, born at the same time

Twinkle
A Yorkshire penis

fig.359 Twig

Tt

Twirled
Yorkshire

Twist
Yorkshire card game

Twofold
Beginners' origami class

Typhoon
Tea that gives you wind

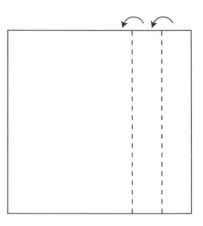

fig.360 Twofold

Tyrannosaurus
A dictator with tender buttocks

Tyrant
 1. An ant that works for Kwik Fit
 2. Angry reaction to being told you have to wear a tie

Uu Vv

fig.361 Venezuela

Uu Vv

U-bend
What you do for the Queen

Über
A very camp exclamation of how cold it is

Uganda
Go and have a look

Umbrage
  1. Angry clash between umbrella users
  2. Card game for the hesitant

Umlaut
Yob who can't make his mind up

Uncoil
A French contraceptive

fig.362 U-bend

Undertaker
 1. A half-hearted shoplifter
 2. Someone who nicks your pants

Undeterred
A skidmark

Unfettered
Without Greek cheese

Ungrateful
A blazing fire in France

Unification
A dodgy French holiday

fig.363 Uniform

Uniform
Having the shape of a female sheep

Unilever
A stick for getting students out of bed

Uu Vv

Unisex
What students have when they're up at university

United
'Arise, Sir Lancelot!'

Unkempt
The process by which Spandau Ballet split up

Unscrew
French prison warder

Untidy
Let Jack loose

Upsadaisy
Flower fetishist

fig.364 Urinate

Urdu
What you get in a Liverpool branch
of Toni & Guy

Urethra
A soul singer who takes the piss

Urinate
You're not a size seven

Usury
Japanese for 'usually'

fig.365 Unscrew

Vaccinate
To administer drugs with a hoover

Vacillate
A tardy lubricant

Vanilla
A large white ape

fig.366 Vanilla

Uu Vv

Vanish
Rather like a van

Variation
Extremely Indian

Varicose
Nearby

Varnish
To disappear in Surrey

Vegetarian
Bad hunter

Vegetate
Art gallery for greengrocers

Veneer
Flemish painter of floorboards

fig.367 Veneer

Venezuela
A gondola with a harpoon

Verbatim
A word to Tim

Veritude
Well munched

Vespa
Evensong on a scooter

Victory
A Conservative MP you can rub on your chest

Vigilant
An insect that stays up all night

Vigilante
An old relative who stays up all night

fig.368 Vigilant

Uu Vv

Violin
Nasty pub

Virgin broadband
A chaste female musical group

Virgin olive oil
Popeye's fiancé

Vocation
Giving your voice a rest

fig.369 Violin

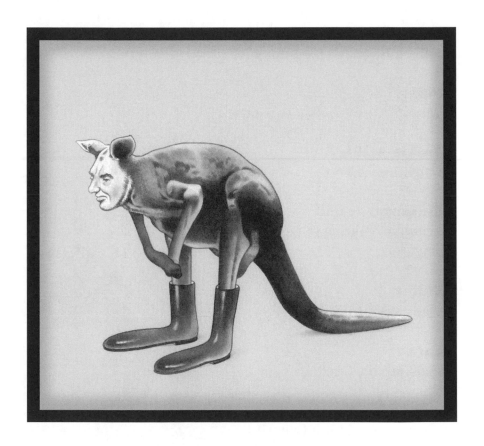

fig.370 Wallaby

Ww

Wagtail
Colleen Rooney's biography

Waif
Spouse *cf. 'you'll have met the waif?'*

Walkie-talkie
A flightless parrot

Wallaby
Someone aspiring to be a
kangaroo

Wallet
A lady wall

Walnut
An obsessive bricklayer

Walrus
Last exclamation of Russell's
driving instructor

Warbling
Geordie jewellery

fig.371 Warehouse

Wagtail – Waxwork

Warehouse
A person who turns into a
house at the full moon

Warming
Geordie porcelain

Warthogs
Geordie clothing

Washington
A substantial amount of laundry

Wassail
What Nelson said when he put the
telescope to his blind eye

Wastrel
A very idle bird of prey

Waxwork
Slogan for the Society for the
Restoration of Corporal
Punishment

fig.372 Washington

fig.373 Wastrel

Ww

WC2
Downstairs cloakroom

Website
The distance between a web
and the ground

Weeding
The sound made by a very
small Scottish handbell

Weight-machine
A Southern Rail train

Welfare
Blonde, innit

Wench
A spanner belonging to Jonathan Ross

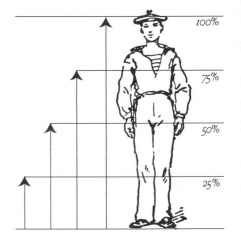

fig.374 Wholesaler

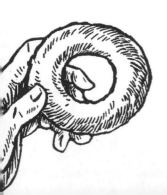

fig.375 Wholefood

Whiff
Noise made by a posh dog

Whimsical
A harvesting tool to be used when the mood takes you

Whipper-snapper
A photographer for an S&M magazine

Whisky
A bit like a whisk

Wholefood
A doughnut

Wholesaler
Moby Dick's lunch

Why-aye
Geordie broadband

Wicked
Evil cricket equipment

fig.376 Weeding

Ww

Wickerwork
Overseas TV journalism

Widdicombe
A brush to make your hair look like a wig

Wide-eyed
Coroner's report

Wifi
The eye of a wife

Wikileaks
What happens when you use a basket as a urinal

Willie-nillie
Cycling accident

fig.377 Wikileaks

Windbreak
Backward fart

Windscreen
Underpants

Winnebago
A horse with a bad back

fig.378 Winnebago

Winsome
Partial success

Wisp
A really pathetic wasp

Wisteria
A nostalgic form of panic

Witchcraft
Consumer magazine for boat owners

fig.379 Wisp

Ww

Wolverine
A product for cleaning wolves

Wonder
The period before Tudor

Woodpecker
Low-cost penis replacement

Working
A Geordie's monarch

Wormcast
A downloadable worm

Worsted
Unpopular bear

Wristwatch
All-night vigil in a very
strict monastery

fig.380 Woodpecker

fig.381 Worsted

fig.382 Zebra

Xx Yy Zz

Xenophobia
Fear of Buddhists

Xerox
Jeffrey Archer's typewriter

X-rated
No longer appreciated

X-ray
Former fish

Xylophone
The Greek goddess of Scrabble

Yacht
A negative yes

Yankee
One who is yanked

fig.383 Xenophobia

Yard
Used to do pirate impressions

Yardage
Three feet old

Yarmouth
A flavoured wine from Norfolk

Yeoman
Presidential greeting

Yo!
A yoyo that only goes one way

Yodelling
Trainee Jedi knight

fig.384 Yo!

Xx Yy Zz

Yonder
One who yonds

Yule log
Mr Brynner has left without flushing

Zebra
The largest size of support garment

Zinc
To zubmerge beneath the zea

fig.385 Zinc

Zip-a-dee-doo-dah
What to do before leaving the gents

Zither
Yorkshire for 'look here'

Zucchini
Animal park enthusiast

fig.386 Zucchini

Foreign Words & Phrases

fig.387 Trompe l'oeil

Foreign Words & Phrases

A cappella
The band hasn't turned up

Ad hoc
Liven up your rice pudding with a little German wine

Ad nauseam
Latest Go Compare campaign

À la carte
A Muslim wheelbarrow

Alter ego
A priest who's full of himself

Annus horribilis
Do you mind if I don't sit down?

Après midi d'une faune
You've been on the phone since lunch

fig.388 À la carte

Après nous le deluge
The lavatory's blocked

Après ski
I've finished the yoghurt

Au clair de la lune
Claire's a bit of a nutter

Avant garde
Next to last coach on the train

Avez-vous faim?
Would you like my sister?

Beaujolais nouveau
Unsuitable for drinking

Belle époque
A cheap cut of pig meat

Bona fide
That's a genuine dog

fig.389 Avez-vous faim?

Foreign Words & Phrases

Bureau de change
Superman's telephone box

Cannelloni al forno
Al's fallen in the canal

Carpe diem
Fish of the day

C'est la guerre
Nautical outfits

Chacun à son goût
Oh you like Pot
Noodle do you?

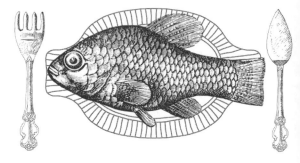

fig.390 Carpe diem

Con allegro
A second-hand car salesman

Corps anglais
French blokes lusting after English women

Cul de sac
My bag is in the refrigerator

Dieu et mon droit
Margaret Thatcher's family motto: 'God and me are right'

Dim sum
Turn the lights down a bit

Donna è mobile
A portable kebab stand

Donner und blitzen
The after-effects of a kebab

Droit de seigneur
The gents is on the right

Et in arcadia ego
I had an omelette down the
shopping precinct

fig.391 C'est la guerre

Et tu Brute
Blimey you've splashed it on all over and no mistake

Foreign Words & Phrases

Fiat lux
Car wash

Film noir
Oh damn! The holiday
photos haven't come out

Fin de siècle
Bicycle lover

Grand prix
Donald Trump

Haiku
A greeting among pigeons

Hande hoch!
The white wine is at your elbow!

Hara-kiri
An opera singer educated
at public school

fig.392 Fiat lux

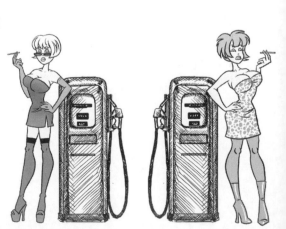

fig.393 Hors d'oeuvre

Fiat lux – La belle dame sans merci

Hors d'oeuvre
Ladies who hang around diesel pumps

Ich bin ein Berliner
I am a bin liner

Ich dien
I am Jayne Torvill's dancing partner

Ich liebe dich
I'm very fond of Richard

Infra dig
I'm an archaeologist

In loco parentis
Dad's an engine driver

La belle dame sans merci
The operator never says thank you

fig.394 Infra dig

Foreign Words & Phrases

La vie en rose
A pink toilet

Laissez faire
To use your discount travel card in Paris

Magnum opus
Tom Selleck's Irish cat

Mens sana in corpore sano
Corporal punishment is available in the men's sauna

Mi casa tu casa
My house has two lavatories

Moi aussi
I am an Australian

Non compos mentis
I don't think that's
meant to be fertiliser

fig.395 Mi casa tu casa

La vie en rose – Sole mio

Petite chose
Your flies are
undone

Pince nez
Not wearing
underwear

Prima donna
Guy Ritchie's
bachelor days

fig.396 Sole mio

Requiescat in pacem
Our cat was totally ruined in the park

Sang froid
'I'm Dreaming of a White Christmas'

Sic transit gloria mundi
Gloria was sick in the van but she'll be in on Monday

Sole mio
That's my fish

Foreign Words & Phrases

Spaghetti carbonara
My dinner's on fire

Steak tartare
The meat's off

Sub judice
The Israeli underground system

fig.397 Spaghetti carbonara

Tant pis, tant mieux
Auntie's been to the bathroom and
she's feeling much better now

Trompe l'oeil
Ooh, that one made my eyes water

Tutti frutti
Baked beans

Veni, vidi, vici
I came to see Vicky;
unfortunately she
was suffering from a
social disease

fig.398 Vin ordinaire

Vin ordinaire
Ford Transit

🅰bbreviations

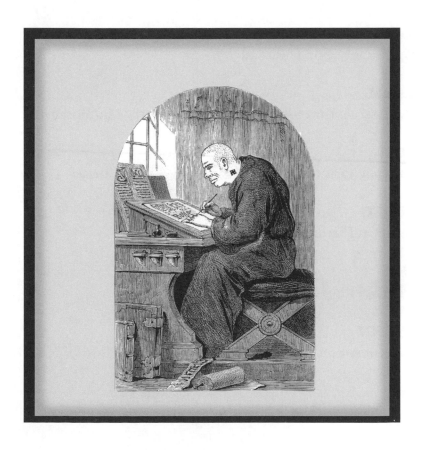

fig.399 NFMPS

Abbreviations

AAAA
The Society For The Deaf

AABM
The Association for the Abolition of Barry Manilow

CIEC
Campaign for the Impregnation of Edwina Curry

COPEC
Colin On Piano Empties Concert halls

CSK
Keep Spelling Correct

CSRHH
The Conservative Sisterhood for the Re-election of Herr Hitler

EU
Yorkshire expression of admiration

MSUL
Marks & Spencer's Underwear Leaks

NFMPS
National Front Medieval Poetry Society

RFCMC
Radio Four Can Murder Comedy

USB
North American Insect

USWD
Unbearably Sexy Winter Drawers

fig.400 USB